The Warren Court's Conceptions of Democracy

The Warren Court's Conceptions of Democracy

An Evaluation of the Supreme Court's Apportionment Opinions

Howard Ball

RUTHERFORD ● MADISON ● TEANECK
Fairleigh Dickinson University Press

Associated University Presses, Inc.
Cranbury, New Jersey 08512

ISBN: 0-8386-7913-7
Printed in the United States of America

For my girls:
Carol
Susan
Sheryl

Contents

Figures

Tables

Preface

In this critical study of the Supreme Court, two basic theoretical questions were raised and discussed with regard to the Court's apportionment opinions: (1) What were the various conceptions of democracy and of representative government expressed by the justices; and (2) which of these conceptions could be judged to be *reasonable*, given the democratic notions of "fallibilism," "open-endedness," and incremental changes in social and economic programs.

The study was initiated because it was felt that a study of the normative basis of Court opinions—and an examination of the structure of the opinions—was important of itself. There have been many books written about judicial process, impact of Court opinions, etc., but none, to my knowledge, has examined—critically (with the use of an evaluative paradigm) —the normative aspect of Supreme Court opinions. In preparing this study I was fortunate enough to speak at length with sitting justices of the United States Supreme Court. Through these interviews I was better able to understand how they were able to formulate the ideas they presented in the Apportionment cases. In reading this book, one must not lose sight of the fact that the Court is being examined for its normative political philosophy output.

Acknowledgments

So many people have helped me complete the research project; thanks are in order at this time. So, thanks to Herb Rosenbaum and Tom Lauth at Hofstra University, for their criticism and their prodding, especially Herb's suggestion that I pick up the pencil. At Rutgers University, thanks to Ben Baker and Neil McDonald, who understood some of the problems I faced, and encouraged me when things looked darkest. And most special thanks to Jay Sigler, my Ph.D. Chairman, who, through terribly good criticism and tough prodding, accomplished what others had failed to do. Miscellaneous thanks to Bob Getz, State University at Brockport, for his encouragement and kind words in the Spring of 1969, to my colleagues for having to listen to my ideas and look at my paradigms, to the Justices of the Supreme Court, especially Mr. Justice Hugo L. Black who was so kind to me, for allowing me to interview them, and to my wife, Carol, for putting up with me in those dark years. To all these people, and so many more, thanks.

HOWARD BALL
Hempstead, New York

The Warren Court's
Conceptions of Democracy

1

The Framework for the Examination

INTRODUCTION

In its apportionment cases, the Supreme Court majority created new political and legal relationships with its decisions. All Court decisions are actions that lead to some form of reaction in the legal, social, and political environment: the apportionment decisions made law for a particular situation and elicited counter-actions from other agencies of government—on both the national and the state levels. This study focuses on but two of the many important questions that arose when the Court entered the apportionment controversy: (1) What were the conceptions of democracy and of representative government expressed by the justices? (2) Which of the opinions, if any, could be called reasonable?

If, however, judges are not professional moral philosophers and if their opinions do not exhibit the craftsmanship associated with such scholars, can such an evaluation of their product be undertaken? Though not claiming to have the qualities of "a detached and somewhat godlike observer,"[1] the author believes that such evaluation can

21

be undertaken and the purpose of this project is to provide a critical examination of a number of Supreme Court apportionment opinions.

At its best, a judicial decision is "an act proceeding from practical reason, that is, a rational action."[2] If the judges do not exhibit good reasons to justify their actions, or do not exhibit any reasons, then that opinion is irrational or, in the latter instance, nonrational. An evaluation of the Supreme Court's apportionment opinions will, in large measure, be an examination of the nature and the dimensions of these reasons offered (if any were offered) by the judges to justify their actions.

Evaluating the reasonableness or unreasonableness of these opinions means examining statements written (collectively) by political men who "lack the time to indulge in subtle philosophic calculations."[3] It also means establishing criteria for such an evaluation that take into account the time element as well as the "fluidity of judicial choice"[4] that is present in "opinion-creation" due to the situational context and due also to the nature of the judges themselves.

Establishing the criteria to judge the reasonableness of judicial actions must be based on an understanding of the nature of the Supreme Court opinion in general, abstract terms. Without such an understanding, the evaluator cannot adequately understand a process that, to begin with, evidences a "potential disparity between a highly fluid input stage and a relatively, simplistic official output."[5]

Because of its importance, the following section of this chapter will deal with the general dimensions of the judicial opinion. After this short discussion, the final segment of the chapter will outline and discuss the criteria that will be used in the evaluation of the apportionment opinions.

I. THE JUDICIAL OPINION: NORMATIVE JUDGMENT OF THE COURT

a. The Nature of Policy-Making

Policy-making necessitates "choices among contesting value systems," and, because this element of choice is constant, when making political decisions, "the ethical dimension is always ubiquitous."[6] Those who are involved in political decision-making are always categorizing—drawing lines. Their task is to make classifications (prescriptions) essential to the orderly functioning and progress of the society. In so doing, the policy-makers are deciding who is equal to whom and who is unequal in a given category: "more crudely, who is to get what."[7] And in this choice "the question of what is arbitrary and capricious (and what is equitable and just; reasonable or unreasonable) is an elusive matter when it comes to passing on the legality or a classification."[8]

For purposes of this evaluation, the output of judicial policy-making, the decision (the judicial opinion) is seen as a complex, organic whole consisting of and reflecting, in various degrees of complexity, three major interdependent dimensions or phases.[9] In policy-making there has to be a definition of the empirical situation, and so the first phase is the *Moral Dimension* of the decision—the conceptual framework—used to frame the set of phenomena being dealt with by the political decision-maker.[10] This dimension is "an awareness and formulation of value hierarchies which are to be used" whenever choices have to be made concerning the drawing of lines. "Our values in large measure," wrote Neil Reimer, "guide the problems that we investigate empirically, the data we select, and the appraisals we make of the empirical evidence we have obtained."[11]

The second phase of the decision is the *Empirical Dimension*. This phase encompasses the perception or image of "reality" held by decision-makers, a consequence of their choice of a conceptual framework. The decision-maker's commitment to a value hierarchy colors his picture of reality. Given a particular commitment, the decision-makers will perceive empirical actions in accordance with their hierarchies and will also judge, "technically evaluate," consequences of particular events or choices they have to make in that particular situation.[12]

The consequences of perceiving reality on the basis of a conceptual framework constitutes the third phase of political decision-making: the *Legislative Dimension* (or the response of the evaluator to the situation perceived). This dimension consists of the formulation into law of practical judgments for society; it is the visible output of the political process. The legislative dimension (a) relates primary values to secondary or instrumental ones. That is, judgments may be formulated which attempt to spell out the fundamental principle of democracy by reconciling clashes between various instrumental principles such as the rights of the majority and the rights of the minority, or (b) attempts to implement, when absent, primary and secondary societal values held by the political actors which crystallize their perception of the good life. The legislative dimension therefore justifies, or at least attempts to justify, the actions taken by the policy-makers in that there are good reasons presented to justify the action taken.[13]

b. The Dimensions of a Judicial Opinion

The Supreme Court's opinions concerned with the issue of apportionment, including the initial judgment that there was or was not a justiciable issue presented to the Courts, were based on various judicial perceptions of the apportionment issue and of the role and the function of the Court in their normative dimensions. The Court, in the process of framing its opinions on a particular case, had to make an initial choice regarding "competing bases of representation—ultimately, really," said Justice Felix Frankfurter, "among competing theories of political philosophy."[14] Justice John M. Harlan, Jr., also participating in the apportionment cases, said that "what lies at the heart of this controversy is a difference of opinion as to the function of representative government."[15] This choice, this difference of opinion over competing conceptual frameworks regarding the nature of democracy and of representative government—the normative dimension—becomes the conceptual spectacles through which the Court judges perceive reality (the empirical dimension) and make their choices known (the legislative dimension).

The written opinion of the Court is the outward manifestation of a judge's commitment to a particular value hierarchy; it is the three phases of policy-making organically welded together. It is the classificatory device used by the Court majority to express and to possibly justify a particular conceptual framework through an instant, empirical political event or series of events. Given this commitment to a particular conception (of democracy, for example), a course of action is chosen because the majority of the Court feels that that particular course will achieve better than any alternative courses open to the Court the greatest amount of good in the quest for the better life.

"A decision," Lon Fuller once wrote, "involves two things; a set of words and an objective sought. The objective may not be happily expressed in the words chosen by the legislator or the judge; it may be perceived dimly or clearly, but it is always present."[16] The roots of Court behavior lie in the "objectives sought" by these men and in the conceptual framework of the judges lies the roots of reasonableness or unreasonableness.

"Facts" surrounding the apportionment controversy are viewed by the Supreme Court justices in the light of the normative dimension acceptable to a Court majority. (This involves the intricate working out of an agreement by, say, six judges, of one particular conceptual framework that somehow reflects the values of the whole group.) "The facts in litigation are the most elusive elements in human conduct. That they may not be found by push-button techniques is not worthy of serious consideration," as Justice William O. Douglas has said, "The words of the Constitution gain meaning and content from the value judgments one puts into them. These value judgments," Douglas concludes, "are not those for robots."[17]

The Supreme Court is not, however, a collective Platonic wise man. In making decisions, the Court functions as one of the many centers of political control in the American political universe. The majority opinion of the

Court then, given their commitment to a particular value hierarchy and their desire to do good and to seek an objective (former Justice Arthur J. Goldberg once said that "the moral imperative of the Court is the advancement of equal justice between men and the achievement of this great goal of the society"[18]), "have to take into account not only the scope and source of their power and the instruments available to them, but also the restrictions on their power and the points at which these restraints could be most damagingly applied."[19] The Court's commitment to a conceptual framework, therefore, has to be formulated or somehow take into account "the simple and overweening fact that any judge's perception of justice is shaped by the social milieu in which he works."[20]

Given the moral dimension, the importance of the conceptual framework, one gets a better view of the "facts" presented by the judges in their opinions—the empirical dimension of decision-making. After using the conceptual framework to "technically evaluate" the empirical situation, there is the legislative dimension: the formulation of policy statements by the Court judges which respond to the controversy by discussing possible choices open to the Court, and the reasons justifying a particular choice reached by the judges in their opinion. These judgments can either state that there is no disagreement between conceptual framework and empirical reality or that there is some disagreement—a gap—between conceptual framework and reality and then state the manner in which the situation contradicts the theory. If the latter situation exists, the Court's judgments contain prescriptive orders which would hopefully (in the judgment of the Court majority), if implemented, narrow the gap between theory and reality.

II. CRITERIA FOR EXAMINING AND EVALUATING JUDICIAL OPINIONS

Working with the tripartite division of a decision concept, the crucial stage in an evaluation of these opinions of the Court is the establishing of criteria for the examination. Professor Eugene Meehan, writing in *Contemporary Political Thought: A Critical Study,* maintains that there are three basic points that should be examined as they appear in a normative judgment, that is, a Supreme Court opinion in this study. These are (1) the adequacy of the *definition of the situation as provided by the value hierarchy* (the conceptual framework), (2) the adequacy of the *technical evaluations* on which the normative judgment rests and (3) the adequacy of the *terms of the justifications* presented by the decision-makers, that is, the supporting conclusions.[21]

The series of characteristics and criteria that follow are based on these three general points. Criteria that deal with the adequacy of the definition of the situation as provided for by the judge's conceptual framework focus on (1) *the nature of the conceptual framework* expressed and employed, explicitly or implicitly, by the judges in the various opinions. Describing in this study the various conceptions of democracy and representative government as expressed by the judges is important in evaluating the Court's actions. (Evaluating these theories will call for the creation of a "reasonable" model of democracy and therefore, at the end of this section of the chapter, a brief paradigm of democracy will be presented, based on a book, *The Logic of Democracy* by Thomas L. Thorson.) One element of these conceptual frameworks developed by the judges becomes another criterion to be examined and that is (2) the *situational context* within which all men—political and nonpolitical—operate. "Fallibilism" as a fundamental basis of democracy and of governing in a democracy, will be shown to be an important element in the forthcoming model of democracy.

FIGURE ONE

The Three Dimensions of a Judicial Decision
Reynolds v. Sims—Visible Manifestation

a. *Normative Dimension*
Conceptual Frameworks present:
1. commitment a' (Warren opinion)
2. commitment b' (Harlan opinion)
3. commitment c' (Stewart opinion)
4. commitment d' (Clark opinion)

b. *Empirical Dimension*
Technical Evaluation of set of phenomena in light of (a) :
1. "facts" in light of a'
2. "facts" in light of b'
3. "facts" in light of c'
4. "facts" in light of d'

c. *Legislative Dimension*
Course of action chosen and expressed in opinion, justified or not, in light of (a) and (b) :
1. Majority opinion (Decision of the Court)
2. Dissenting opinion
3. Concurring opinion
4. Concurring opinion

Reynolds v. Sims, 377 *US* 533

When using the term "fallibilism" in discussing the criteria to be applied in the evaluation of the Court's apportionment opinions, and when discussing the adequacy of the judges' perceptions (and their descriptions) of reality, the author is also suggesting that uncertainties in the interpretation of fact-situations are always present and that a reasonable conceptual framework and, therefore, an adequate description of reality will not lose account of the fact of open-endedness. "Our handicaps are the relative ignorance of fact, our relative indeterminacy of aim," and the impossibility of mechanically following rules, wrote H. L. A. Hart. "The open texture of the law," he wrote, "means that there are areas of conduct where much must be left to be developed by courts or officials striking a balance, in the light of circumstances, between competing interests which vary in weight from case to case."[22]

The second set of criteria concern the adequacy of the various "technical evaluations" the judges made in the apportionment opinions, based on their conceptual frameworks. These criteria are: (1) the adequacy of the *perceived consequences* as seen and stated by the judges; (2) the use of *all available data* in the technical evaluation[23]; (3) *due consideration, fairness* and *impartiality* shown by the judges toward all sides in the dispute, and (4) whether all *facets* of the issue were explored by the judges.[24]

The third set of criteria pertain to the legislative dimension of the judicial opinion and concern the adequacy of the terms of the justifications presented by the judges in the apportionment opinions.

The evaluation will also examine whether or not there is seen in the opinions the use of reliable, self-consistent methods in reaching the *conclusion*.

"A rational, just action," wrote Charles Perelman, "is one which is in conformity with a chain of practical reasoning, fidelity to rules, and obedience to the system."[25] Rationality refers to the process of action, the means used to reach a particular choice, not the end in of itself. "A decision may be right yet not rational; wrong and rational," says John Ladd. One has to distinguish between a rational, yet wrong, decision and a correct, (good) though nonrational, decision.[26] An irrational action is one in which acts are performed that are unsuitable for reaching a predetermined aim. Irrationality occurs when "an outrageous price" is paid for an end; "to fail to be reasonable is to advocate and act upon our principles with a degree of conviction out of proportion to their desirability."[27]

Another criterion in this last set is: that there should be *good reasons* offered as justifiable explanations for the choice made by the judges. Reasonable arguments must support a conclusion reached; if there are no reasons offered, there is no justification, no evaluation. An opinion without supporting reasons is simply a nonrational one.[28] Good reasons can indicate reasonableness; bad ones make it irrational. What are good reasons? Rationality is related to the context of a particular system and to the type of problem being dealt with. "Canons of rationality, the determination of what is to be accepted as a good reason and rejected as a bad reason, are established within the discipline itself," says John Ladd.[29] Thus a good reason would be one that follows, however imperfectly (given the open-endedness of the laws and man's fallibility), standards of legal and political rationality. In short, the Courts operate in a larger political universe; they are limited with respect to the nature of the commands they give and the means of enforcing these prescriptions. (This accounts for the stress placed on the *situational context* criterion. Judges are, to repeat, not detached Platonic wise men; there may even be an insoluble conflict between what the judges think is just and what society thinks is just—with society's thoughts overcoming those of the Court.)

Edmond Cahn once wrote that the judge's most difficult task is to "adjust moral standards to the level that society can aspire to attain."[30] That he is not always going to be successful is an attitude that the reasonable judge possesses; it is the unreasonable judge who "acts" on his principles "with a degree of conviction out of proportion to their desirability." In this difficult task of adjusting moral standards that Cahn writes about—in effect, interpreting the Constitution and statutes in light of a particular conceptual framework—legal precedent is followed *only by showing* that the following of precedent does less harm than any possible alternative course of action.[31] Concerning questions of constitutional law, the role of precedent may lose its significance in the minds of a majority of judges. As Professor Sigler states: the need for homeostasis in the legal system may be sacrificed for the greater needs of the political and social system for homeostasis. H. L. A. Hart, in a similar vein, said that "a good reason for a judicial act is the validity of the basic principle of law in question (given all the handicaps that go along with the "open texture" of the laws)."[32]

But there is the prior act of judging whether the basic principle of law in question applies, holds, or is valid in a particular case and setting. The "mechanism" of legal reasoning, differing from the "pretense" of legal reasoning, is the acceptance of "differences of view and ambiguities of words" because "legal rules are never clear. . . . The basic pattern of legal reasoning is reasoning by example. It is reasoning from case to case," writes Edward Levi.[33] He continues, saying that legal reasoning is a three-step process: "similarity is seen between cases; next, the rule of law inherent in the first case is announced; then the rule of law is made applicable to the second case."[34] And, in this process, it is the judge who must determine (as Hart points out) the validity of the law in question before it is applied to the instant case under discussion.

Ideally, then, in a reasonable judicial opinion written about the apportionment controversy, a judge would:

(1) have a theory of democracy and representative government (conceptual framework) that is viable insofar as it enables the perceiver to take into account changes in the situational context, human fallibility, and it allows the perceiver to adequately define the situation facing him as judge;

(2) in "technically evaluating" the situation, use all available data, show fairness and consideration to all sides in the dispute (as Ladd writes, "rationality, in part, consists in the agent's paying some heed to the claims of alternative courses of action" and that the judge "reaches a rational decision after giving due consideration to both sides of the dispute."[35]), and, in coming to his decision, indicate what he perceives to be consequences of alternative courses of action open to him;

(3) justify his action (decision) by presenting (self-consistent) reasons, good reasons, and presenting them in a way that does not belittle or demean those who read it.

FIGURE TWO
Criteria for Evaluating a Judicial Opinion

Criteria

I. *Definition of the Situation as Provided by the Conceptual Framework—the Value Hierarchy*
   a. Nature of Conceptual Framework
   b. Awareness of Situational Context
      1. political-social system
      2. human "fallibilism"
   c. Adequacy of the perceived situation

II. *The Technical Evaluation*
   a. Perceived consequences
   b. Use of available data
   c. Due consideration evidenced
   d. Structure of the evaluation

III. *Terms of the Justification*
   a. Self-consistent methods used to reach conclusion
      1. practical reasoning
      2. fidelity to rules
   b. Good reasons offered for the action
      1. follow standards of legal and political rationality
   c. Respect for a person's rationality evidenced

Reynolds v. Sims—Visible manifestation

a. *Normative Dimension*
   Conceptual Frameworks present:
   1. commitment a′ (Warren opinion)
   2. commitment b′ (Harlan opinion)
   3. commitment c′ (Stewart opinion)
   4. commitment d′ (Clark opinion)

b. *Empirical Dimension*
   Technical Evaluation of set of phenomena in light of (a):
   1. "facts" in light of a′
   2. "facts" in light of b′
   3. "facts" in light of c′
   4. "facts" in light of d′

c. *Legislative Dimension*
   course of action chosen and expressed in opinion, justified or not, in light of (a) and (b):
   1. Majority opinion (Decision of the Court)
   2. Dissenting opinion
   3. Concurring opinion
   4. Concurring opinion

   Reynolds v. Sims, 377 US 533

Important as all these criteria are, one criterion stands out above the others, and that criterion is the conceptual framework applied by the judge in these apportionment opinions. As indicated, the conceptual framework frames reality for the perceiver. For the purposes of this study, a paradigm of democracy is to be constructed that, if replicated, would lead to a reasonable opinion in that other criteria of reasonableness, outlined above, would be followed. A reasonable model of democracy should comport with the aforementioned criteria; that is, it should reflect the situational context, it should accept the open-endedness of the laws and the necessity of changes due to past errors, it should aim for the alleviation of suffering and for the attainment of the good life for all, it should stress the importance of good reasons, and rest on due consideration shown all citizens.

Earlier in the chapter it was mentioned that decisions involve goals sought by policy-makers, and that the goal sought by the Supreme Court judges was the narrowing of the gap between conceptual frameworks, theories—in the apportionment cases, of democracy—and reality. In a sense, the judges, by attempting to narrow the separation between reality and professed goals, are acting to maintain legal standards—due process, fair trial—and political norms —representative government, democracy, majority rule, minority rights. The theory the judges hold of democracy and of representative government becomes the crucial factor in the evaluation of judicial opinions. What follows is a brief model of democracy.

III. A MODEL OF A DEMOCRATIC CONCEPTUAL FRAMEWORK

We have already indicated that political behavior is open to choices among alternative courses of action, and choice "is a process by which we scan a number of possible futures, allot some ordinal numbers such as first, second, third to elements of this set, and pick out the element which is labeled first."[36] In this picking, the judge works with a particular conceptual framework. It is preferable that he will decide wisely given the situational context. He will decide reasonably if his theory of democracy stresses fallibility and open-endedness.

a. Democracy as a Principle of Governing Men

"All life is an experiment," wrote Justice Oliver Wendell Holmes, Jr. in a 1919 Supreme Court decision,[37] and democracy, as a fundamental principle of governing men, reflects this idea to the fullest extent possible. Democracy's basic assumption is that "all men stand on an equal footing of ignorance regarding the ultimate meaning of life."[38] The categorical imperative of democracy as a principle of governing is a simple one: "Do not block the way of inquiry and of change with regard to social and economic matters."[39] The risks of democracy "are simply the risks implicit in suggesting to men that the answers are not all in."[40] Inherent in this fundamental principle of governing is a view of human nature that accepts the fallibility, imperfection, and error-proneness of man; a view that assumes man's lack of total knowledge about "reality" and lack of discernability about what is best for himself and for society.[41] (As former Chief Justice Earl Warren said recently, policy-makers "are not monks or scientists, but participants in the living stream of our national life."[42] As such, they are expected to make mistakes; a democratic system must allow for such errors and allow for the changes that should follow once errors are uncovered.)

Democracy "has little to say about the substantive content of the economic or social theories that prevail."[43] The principle of democracy merely provides a democratically oriented social system with a mechanism constructed by men on the basis of democracy's instrumental principles; that is, those values, such as "majority rule," and "minority rights," that spell out the fundamental democratic principle through which the wishes of the society can be continuously reflected and modified in light of further acquisition of knowledge. A society is democratic *only if* men can live with the risks it implies.

b. The Practical Spelling Out of the Principle

Given the situational context of man—equality in terms of ignorance—democracy's institutional values (majority rule, minority rights, political equality, free expression of ideas, due process and equal protection of the laws guarantees) guide society in establishing a particular mechanism of governing. This mechanism reflects the democratic principle and is constructed so that *institutionally* no one man or group can claim a monopoly of power on the grounds that they have all the answers; as a result, there is no need for further discussion (free speech) on social and economic issues.[44] On the contrary, these institutional values allow for imperfection, allow for errors to be made and corrected within a social system. They set up a mechanism, a political system, consisting of a series of practical devices concerning (1) the type of structure (federal, unitary), (2) the *methods* (procedures, agents) used to create acts and control behavior, and (3) the *limits* of control behavior in a democratic society. The mechanism will not function for long *demo-*

cratically without various procedures for allowing individuals and groups to voice their views on issues that
affect them. Man's state of knowledge calls for a system
that allows and protects human rights—especially the
functional civil and political freedoms of speech, expression, and petition of grievances—in order that the will
of the people be expressed and acted upon by those in the
political system. Thus the democratic political system, constructed on the basis of instrumental principles of democracy, is a process that combines the principle of democracy
and the principle of human rights. "Together [they]
create a system which allows for man's fallibility and
weakness. Together they create a self-corrective mechanism
which permits all manner of social experiment and yet
provides for the continuing accommodation of mankind's
emerging needs."[45]

(1) Majority Rule and Minority Rights

Democracy assumes majority rule. As President Abraham Lincoln said, in his first inaugural address,[46]

> A majority held in restraint by constitutional checks
> and limitations, and always changing easily with de-
> liberate changes of popular opinions and sentiments,
> is the only true sovereign of a free people. Whoever
> rejects this does, of necessity fly to anarchy or despotism.
> Unanimity [in governing] is impossible; the rule of a
> minority as a permanent arrangement is wholly im-
> possible; so that, rejecting the majority principle, an-
> archy or despotism in some form is all that is left.

As the statement implies, majority rule "held in restraint"
is the only practical solution open to a society that opts
for a democratic political system. The concept of majority

rule is a difficult one to spell out in a society of 200 million citizens and, in itself, it is not an absolute value. Any argument for absolute majority rule "is specious and the position in its categorical form is utterly without justification" simply because there is no way to justify decisions made in the name of democracy which deny a minority of its citizens the right to vote, freedom of speech, freedom of assembly, and freedom of the press in order to serve the interests of the majority.[47] If "the intellectual rationale of democracy is precisely that it does not need to make the foolish and arrogant claim that it rests on infallible truths,"[48] and if the principle of democracy assumes open-ended and pragmatic judgments to be the natural qualities of policy-making, then the mechanism, the political system, has to allow for the possibility of minorities altering majorities' social and economic policies (or, at the very least, minorities using devices and agencies to suggest possible alternatives and modifications in existing public policies).

In a social system consisting of 200 million people, in a social system with great diversities (geographical, demographic, economic, cultural, religious), the always-existing tensions between the instrumental principles of majority rule and minority rights are heightened even more. The political mechanism developed and constructed by our political leaders, federalism, attempts to deal with diversity as well as with the problem of majority and minority rights and obligations.

A federal political system, assuming diversity, creates multiple centers of power. Rather than one unitary center within which deliberate control acts are made for the society, federalism divides a social system into smaller sovereign political entities (states). Within these smaller political systems, a further division occurs. Control acts involve law-making, law-enforcing, and law-adjudication agents and agencies in these systems. There is also a control mechanism for the national social system, for implicit in the idea of federalism is the view that the states are organically welded together to form the national union and the latter,[49] to function properly, must also make and enforce control acts for the good of the larger society (or rather, for the individual within the states, who is also a citizen of the larger, more remote, national political control system).

The American version of democracy is one example of a society's accepting and then, given the physical situational context, spelling out practically that principle of governing. If one views democracy as essentially a system of mutual deference or mutual respect, a system where citizens are appreciated, consulted, taken into consideration, share in power and generally feel that they somehow (through various associations they make and belong to) participate in the construction of social and economic decisions,[50] then a form of pluralistic democracy is most appropriate for such a diverse social system.

Pluralistic democracy stresses the importance of groups within the political system. The sovereign majority, seen as a set of minorities, that is, smaller groups aligned together on an issue, is held in restraint and limited in such a structure; opportunities for other minorities to present their ideas on matters of importance and for negotiations to take place between various groups—and their elected representatives, within certain limits—in order to produce a more constructive and meaningful public policy are built into the political mechanism. In such an environment, conflicts and problems stand a good chance of being resolved peacefully.

Assuming the absence of a homogeneous majority, for example, the "urban voter," and the absence of a permanent minority group that always loses (other than extralegal organizations such as the White Citizens Councils, the Ku Klux Klan, the Minutemen, etc.), "minorities rule." This realistic appraisal of the nature of political activity in our society has been developed as one way to meet the demands of the principle of democracy—if the society wants to meet them. In meeting these demands, another major instrumental principle of democracy, political equality, enters into the discussion of the nature and dimensions of that general principle of governing.

(2) Political Equality

If the majority rule principle is the only practical solution to the fundamental question of "who governs" or who controls in a democracy, then the instrumental principle of political equality is the antecedent concept that determines just who will govern. It means that, excepting citizenship, age, and residency requirements, no criterion —be it wealth, sex, place of residence, race, religion, or intelligence—can justify a denial of one's right to vote and to have that vote counted the same as any other vote. "The ballot box is the democratic process. Equality in voting—one man and every man, one vote—does not, by any means, solve all the problems of democracy, but without it democracy is a sham."[51]

Political equality is essential to the maintenance of a stable, pluralist democratic system because it presupposes competitiveness, visibility, responsiveness, and accessibility for all interests who wish to involve themselves in the formulation, changing, or blocking of public policies. Blocking such access to the political system is antithetical to the logic of the principle of democracy for it could possibly cut off new ideas for ameliorating social conflict and improving the conditions of life in society. In Harold Lasswell's terminology, it can lead to a loss of self-respect and the development of destructive impulses that endanger the fulfillment of the principles of democracy because the "feeling" of being a part of the system has been destroyed.

Accessibility is vital to the continuance of a democratic system. "The likelihood of peaceful adjustment to a conflict," wrote Robert Dahl, "is increased if there exist institutional arrangements that encourage consultation, negotiation, the exploration of alternatives, and the search for mutually beneficial solutions. Conversely, the prospects of deadlock and coercion are increased if institutional arrangements severely inhibit such activities."[52] Federalism, with its centers of local power and decision-making, optimally affords the citizens access to the political process if they want to enter it. Dahl maintains that the "feeling, or appearance of being able to do something about local affairs," is, in itself, an important reason for the existence of local governments.[53]

Feelings of the citizens are important in the maintenance of system stability. It may very well be that the Supreme Court judges, as perhaps the final interpreters of constitutional provisions such as due process and equal protection, have in recent years realized the importance of "appearances." As one scholar put it: "The Court, as guardian of the Constitution, has sometimes served as conscience of the nation; or as a prime source of symbolic leadership."[54] The apportionment cases may very well be an example of judicial activism on behalf of an instrumental value, majority rule or majoritarianism, that a majority of the judges felt had been rejected or ignored by state legislators. As a prime source of symbolic leadership, there would seem to be no contradictions between judicial activism and majoritarianism. The Court was acting to restore a system-wide value to its proper place of importance before the people lost faith in the values of the system.

Apportionment can be the vital determinant in the maintenance of a democratic system. It is the variable that can either restrict or enhance the flow of political communication between interested minorities and the political decision-makers; it is the variable that enunciates the manner in which power will be distributed in a particular political system (national, state, local) —either encouraging or discouraging mutual deference and the feeling or appearance of being consulted and represented.

And in a democratic system, the political system, the mechanism of democracy, has to exhibit the instrumental principles of majority rule, minority rights, and political equality in such a manner so as to ensure a functional and moral commitment to that principle of governing. For these reasons alone, the apportionment controversy is a crucial one for a democratic system. That is why the Supreme Court's response to this issue manifests so clearly a particular conception of the idea of democracy; in order to respond to the issue of apportionment one has to construct or use an existing value hierarchy that reflects a particular commitment to a conception of democracy.

(3) Representativeness

Representation is the political core of any system of political democracy. From what has been already said about democracy, majority rule, minority rights, and political equality, the *"operational necessity"* of majority rule at both the electoral and legislative stages of representation"[55] naturally follows. "Politics," Christian Bay said recently, "exists for the purpose of progressively removing the most stultifying obstacles to a free human development, with priority for the worst obstacles whether they hit many or few."[56] In removing these "stultifying obstacles" fair and effective representation must be present in the legislative assemblies. It must be present because the model of democracy is premised on the idea of "fallibilism" which, translated into political activity, means that political institutions and processes should not block the possibility of change. In discussing a representation system's fairness, optimally there should not be an abuse of power by either the *majority* or the *minority* (or groups of minority interests). A fair and equitable scheme of representation, then, accepts both the idea of responsible majority rule and access to the political system of minorities, minimally (perhaps optimally) through "administrative representation" of these special constituencies or clientele groups[57] by pressure group activity.

In dealing with these problems raised by the apportionment issue, the Supreme Court's avowed goal seems to have been to work out some accommodation between the ideas of "majority rule" and "minority rights." Chief Justice Earl Warren, in the 1964 case of *Reynolds v. Sims,* said that "the achieving of fair and effective representation for all citizens is concededly the basic aim of legislative apportionment." The Court's task has been to examine situations where some blockage has allegedly occurred and resolve these crises.

In dealing with this issue, the Supreme Court's moral dimensions reflect particular conceptions of majority rule, minority rights, political equality, and representativeness that lead to particular consequences for the political system. The conceptual frameworks of the judges will be presented shortly in this study of the Court's reapportionment actions. They will be described and compared with this fallibilism-human ignorance model of democracy. What is to be stressed here, in closing this segment of the chapter, is the open-endedness of democracy: with fallibilism at the foundation, democracy means that, so long as there is the existence within the political structure of means by which interested minorities can participate in public policy making, the substance of the economic and social policies is immaterial. So long as policies do not limit or restrict—unjustly—political actions, democracy means that *anything goes*—until it is proven unsuccessful or until modifications are necessary due to unforeseen difficulties and/or errors that arise after the policy has been adopted and enforced.

IV. THE DESCRIPTION OF THE RESEARCH DESIGN

The purpose of this study is to discuss the Supreme Court's conceptions of democracy and to determine whether or not, on the basis of these conceptions, the Court acted reasonably when it created new legal and political relationships in the aftermath of its apportionment decisions. Put another way, the study will attempt to determine which of these opinions—majority, concurring, or dissenting—were reasonable and which were not. To assist in this evaluation, criteria have been presented which correspond to the three phases of policy-making. Critical to the assessment that is to take place is the normative dimension of the opinions, the judges' conceptual frameworks, in the apportionment cases. Characteristics of democracy have been presented and will be used, for purposes of this study, to compare and evaluate the various views of democracy and representative government pronounced by the justices. The model of democracy here presented, incorporating the criteria, stresses "fallibilism" and "open-endedness" as leading characteristics of a reasonable democratic theory. From these ideas, the categorical imperative of democracy follows: In governing men, do not block the possibility of social change.

The following chapters will contain assessments of three major apportionment cases involving state legislative apportionment that have appeared before the Warren Court: *Baker v. Carr,* 369, *US* 186; *Grey v. Sanders,* 372, *US* 368, and *Reynolds v. Sims,* 377, *US* 533. In addition, there will be an examination of the important 1946 case of *Colegrove v. Green* as well as an examination of some of the post-*Reynolds* decisions of the Supreme Court.

There will be a presentation (1) of the opinions (restructured in light of the preceding discussion of policymaking) , (2) and comparison of the model of democracy used by the judges with the model presented in this chapter. There will be (3) an examination of the (a) adequacy of the definition of the situation, (b) adequacy of the technical evaluation, (c) adequacy of the justifications presented by the judges, and, finally (4) an over-all evaluation of the reasonableness of the opinion.

As indicated above, the critical factor is the theory of democracy used by the judges. If a reasonable approximation of the model of democracy has been presented in the opinion, then the opinion would conceivably ask and answer questions such as: who in society has *actually* (an empirical question) abused power, that is, localized and restrained peaceful conflict over societal goals, the majority? or the minority? If the opinion responds to such a question—if it raises such a question—then, hypothetically, it would tend to lead to a reasonable response—given fallibility and open-endedness.

The assumption made by the author is this: if there is a particular conception of democracy adhered to by the judges, they, in responding to societal conflicts in the form of litigation before the Court, will be aware of the situational context, human fallibilism; they will use all available empirical data, will show due consideration to all facts *that are perceived* by them, and they will offer good reasons for their choice—based upon their fidelity to rules of law and theories of democracy and representative government.

In a sense, this research project is aimed at finding out whether or not the "fallibilistic" concept of democracy has been employed, consciously or not, by a segment of the Supreme Court justices when they responded to sets of phenomena brought to them by citizens. It is the view of the author that such a commitment to this particular conception of democracy, empirically oriented rather than absolutist-theocratic in nature, is a reasonable, rational one and that the society would be greatly benefited if a majority of the judges expressed such a commitment.

NOTES: CHAPTER 1

1. Neil McDonald, *Politics: A Study of Control Behavior*, New Brunswick, Rutgers University Press, 1965, Ch. 2.
2. John Ladd, "The Place of Practical Reason in Judicial Decision," in

Carl Friedrich, editor, *Nomos VII, Rational Decision*, New York, Atherton Press, 1967, p. 127.

3. J. Woodford Howard, Jr., "On the Fluidity of Judicial Choice," LXII *American Political Science Review*, March 1968, p. 50.

4. *Ibid.*

5. *Ibid.*, p. 55.

6. Milford Sibley, in James Charlesworth, ed., *Contemporary Political Analysis*, Glencoe, Free Press, 1967, p. 69.

7. *Ibid.*

8. William O. Douglas, Jr., "The Public Trial and a Free Press," 46 *American Bar Association Journal*, August 1960, p. 845.

9. Sibley, *op cit.*, pp. 69–70.

10. See, Eugene Meehan, *Contemporary Political Thought: A Critical Study*, Homewood, Dorsey Press, 1967, pp. 36–38.

11. Neil Reimer, *The Revival of Democratic Theory*, New York, Appleton-Century-Crofts, 1962, p. 59.

12. Meehan, *op cit.*, p. 41.

13. *Ibid.* and Sibley, *op cit.*, pp. 69–70.

14. *Baker v. Carr*, 369 *US* 186 (1962), at 300.

15. *Ibid.* at 333.

16. Lon Fuller, *The Law in Quest of Itself*, Cambridge, Harvard University Press, 1950, 1962, pp. 8–9.

17. William O. Douglas, Jr., in Edmond Cahn, editor, *The Great Rights*, New York, Macmillan Co., 1963, p. 156.

18. Arthur J. Goldberg, "Gideon's Trumpet: The Poor Man and The Law," *CBS Reports*, October 7, 1964, transcript pages 23–24.

19. Walter Murphy, *Elements of Judicial Strategy*, Chicago, University of Chicago Press, 1965, p. 12.

20. Samuel Krislov, *The Supreme Court in the Political Process*, New York, Macmillan Co., 1965, p. 56.

21. Meehan, *op cit.*, p. 372.

22. H. L. A. Hart, *The Concept of Law*, London, Oxford University Press, 1961, p. 132.

23. See, generally, Abraham Edel, *Science and the Structure of Ethics*, Chicago, University of Chicago Press, 1961.

24. See Ladd, *op cit.*, p. 142.

25. Charles Perelman, *The Idea of Justice*, New York, Humanities Press, 1963, p. 37.

26. Ladd, *op cit.*, p. 128.

27. Stephen Toulmin, *An Examination of the Place of Reason in Ethics*, London, Cambridge, University Press, 1950, pp. 164–165.

28. Ladd, *op cit.*, p. 129, ff.

29. *Ibid.*, p. 142.

30. Edmond Cahn, *The Moral Decision, Right and Wrong in the Light of American Law*, Bloomington, Indiana University Press, 1955, p. 56.
31. Morris Cohen, *Ethical Systems and Legal Ideals*, Ithaca, Cornell University Press, 1933, 1959, p. 33.
32. Hart, *op cit.*, p. 102.
33. Edward Levi, *Introduction to Legal Reasoning*, Chicago, University of Chicago Press, 1948, p. 1.
34. *Ibid.*, p. 2.
35. Ladd, *op cit.*, p. 142.
36. Kenneth Boulding, "Social Justice in Social Dynamics," in Richard Brandt, editor, *Social Justice*, Englewood Cliffs, Prentice-Hall, 1962, p. 75–76.
37. *Schenck v. United States*, 249 US 47 (1919).
38. Durward Sandifer and L. Ronald Scheman, *The Foundations of Freedom*, New York, Praeger and Co., 1965, p. 9.
39. See, generally, Thomas Thorson, *The Logic of Democracy*, New York, Holt, Rinehart, and Winston, 1962.
40. Charles Frankel, *The Democratic Prospect*, New York, Harper and Co., 1962, p. 174.
41. "What is best is not always discernible," wrote Justice William O. Douglas in *Norvell v. Illinois*, 373 US 420 (1961), at 424.
42. Earl Warren, "The Law and the Future," *Fortune*, November 1955, p. 107.
43. Sandifer and Scheman, *op cit.*, p. 16.
44. Thorson, *op cit.*, p. 179.
45. Sandifer and Scheman, *op cit.*, p. 3.
46. Quoted in Thorson, *op cit.*, p. 142.
47. Thomas Thorson, "Epilogue to Absolute Majority Rule," 23 *Journal of Politics*, August 1961, p. 558.
48. Frankel, *op cit.*, p. 179.
49. *Texas v. White*, 7 *Wallace* 700 (1869)
50. Harold Lasswell, "Psychology Looks at Morals and Politics," *Ethics*, April 1941, p. 327, ff; Wm. Riker, *Democracy in the U.S.*, New York: Macmillan, 1961, p. 17, states that "democracy is self-respect for everybody."
51. Leonard Fein, editor, *American Democracy*, New York, Random House, 1965, p. 76.
52. Robert Dahl, *Modern Political Analysis*, Englewood Cliffs, Prentice-Hall, 1963, p. 77.
53. Robert Dahl, *Pluralistic Democracy in the United States*, Chicago, Rand McNally, 1967, p. 200.
54. Jay Sigler, *Introduction to the Legal System*, Homewood, Dorsey Press, 1968, p. 227.

55. William P. Irwin, "Representation and Apportionment: Search for a Theory," in Howard Hamilton, editor, *Reapportioning Legislatures,* Columbus, Charles E. Merrill Books, 1966, p. 139.
56. Christian Bay, "Politics and Pseudopolitics," LIX *American Political Science Review,* March 1965, pp. 49–50.
57. Irwin, *op cit.,* pp. 149–150.

2

The Apportionment Issue
up to Baker v. Carr

INTRODUCTION: THE APPORTIONMENT ISSUE

a. Genesis of the Issue

Action on the part of a minority that deprives other
minorities of their legitimate right to rule is a source of
many conflicts in a democratic society. As a matter of
principle (in line with the model of democracy already
presented), there is no rational way to justify weighing
the preferences of some more heavily than others. "Political philosophy cannot demonstrate in any ultimate sense
that rule by one or by a few is the ideally best form of
government."[1] This does not rule out, as a matter of prac-
ticality, decisions made by a small group due to the need
for speedy action. *Institutionalized* rule by a few is, however, antithetical to the logic of democracy, for it presupposes that only the chosen few are capable of *always* acting
wisely on behalf of the many.

Apportionment goes to the core of the issue of democracy and of *who* are going to represent people in a political system and of *how* they are to be represented. Appor-

51

tionment determines the distribution of political power in state and national legislatures; it is the distribution of seats—legislative representation—within a particular, legally defined, geographical unit. "Whoever decides what the game of politics is about decides also who can get into the game," wrote E. E. Schattschneider,[2] and apportionment, in a sense, is the variable that determines who gets into the game of politics and who will have the power to deliberately control others.

The genesis of the apportionment controversy can be traced back to Colonial America. Political representation at that time was based on locality, regardless of size and importance of the towns, because of the isolation of the communities. By the revolutionary period, the basis of representation had already shifted to the population concept and was accepted, except for the Senate compromise at the 1787 convention, by the Constitutional framers.[3]

During the nineteenth century, apportionment of state legislatures (the legislative seats) based on the population standard became fairly widespread—paralleling the liberalization of suffrage requirements. Due to the sparsity of population in many sections of the nation, however, a casual deviation from this standard was introduced early in this century: all counties were given minimum representation in the state legislatures. In the latter part of the nineteenth century, a deliberate deviation from the population standard took place due to (1) the closing of the frontier, (2) a mobile, growing urban population (in large part) the result of waves of immigration, (3) localism and the accompanying distrust of the city's corrupt bosses and its low-class inhabitants by the rural population and its political leaders, and (4) a desire to preserve the political and economic structure's *status quo*. An imbalance of representation developed, which gradually extended into almost all state legislatures and into the Federal House of Representatives.[4]

Two major factors clearly stand out in explaining the mechanics of the malapportionment that ensued: (1) restrictive constitutional provisions (considered the major source of malapportioned state houses), and (2) legislative inaction where state constitutions called for apportionment at specified times.[5] (See Table I.) A glance at the fifty states' basis of representation indicates that in 1960, the make-up of at least two-thirds of the 99 state houses was based on factors other than population—that is, factors such as weighted population ratios, area, area plus population, fixed constitutional arrangements, and taxation.[6] By 1962, according to one observer, such deviations and complete disregard of the population standard had the practical result of leaving only nine states—Washington, Oregon, South Dakota, Minnesota, Wisconsin, Indiana, Virginia, Massachusetts and Kentucky—"with no constitutional restriction of any consequence upon the fully democratic pattern of popular representation in both houses."[7] (See Table II for 1962 statistics on the extent of malapportionment in the United States.)

Preservation of the status quo—rural political control of the political system—by the politicians, pressure groups, and economic interests from the "urban intruders" was the principal reason for the development of widespread unequal representation in the state houses. Thus, by changing the constitutional standards for apportioning seats, by passing redistricting bills to favor area over population standards, or simply doing nothing if the constitution demanded action on the part of legislators, the immediate political advantage—retention of power and

TABLE I

Basis of Representation, 1962

Basis of Representation		Senate	House
1. "Population"	(32)	Indiana, Kansas, Kentucky, La., Maine, Mass., Minn., Missouri, Nebraska, N. Car., Okla., Oregon, S. Dakota, Tenn., Utah, Va., Wis.	Alaska, Cal., Ill., Indiana, Maine, Mass., Mich., Minnesota, Nevada, N. Hamp., Oregon, S. Dak., Tenn., Va., Wis.
2. Population with Ratios	(5)	Colorado	Colorado, Fla, Georgia, Iowa
3. Population, with Restrictions*	(34)	Ala., Cal., Conn., Fla., Iowa, New York, Pa., R.I., Texas, Vt., Wash., W. Virginia, Wyoming	Ala., Ariz., Hawaii, Idaho, Kansas, Ky., La., New Jersey, New York, N. Car., N. Dak., Ohio, Okla., Pa., R.I., S. Car., Texas, Utah, Wash., W. Va., Wyoming
4. Area, with Population Factors**	(6)	Alaska, Ohio, Maryland	Ark, Conn., New Mexico
5. Area	(11)	Ga., Idaho, Ill, Mont, Nevada, New Jersey, N. Mex., S. Car.	Missouri, Mont., Vt.
6. Taxes	(1)	New Hampshire	
7. Established by Constitution	(10)	Ariz., Ark., Del., Hawaii, Mich., Miss., N. Dak.	Del., Maryland, Mississippi

* Examples: Alabama—"Population, except no district more than one member."
Connecticut—"Population, but each county at least one member."
** Examples: Alaska—"Combination of house districts into four at-large districts and a varying number of minor districts."

b. Malapportioned Legislatures

TABLE II

Maximum Range of Population Differences Among Representation Districts of
State Legislatures, 1962

State Units		Population Mean	Most Populous District	% Over State Average	Least Populous District	% Under	"Min* Maj"
Alabama	(S)	93,335	634,864	580.6	15,417	−83.5	25.1
	(H)	26,497	104,767	240.0	6,731	−78.2	25.7
Alaska	(S)	10,396	57,431	407.9	4,603	−59.3	35.0
	(H)	3,679	6,605	16.8	2,945	−47.9	49.0
Arizona	(S)	46,505	331,755	613.4	3,868	−91.7	12.8
	(H)	16,272	30,438	87.0	5,754	−64.6	− −
Arkansas	(S)	49,024	80,993	58.7	35,983	−29.5	43.8
	(H)	15,926	31,686	77.4	4,927	−72.4	33.3
California	(S)	392,780	6,038,771	1,436.8	14,294	−96.4	10.7
	(H)	195,478	306,191	55.8	72,105	−63.3	44.7
Colorado	(S)	46,176	127,520	154.5	17,481	−65.1	29.8
	(H)	22,070	63,760	136.3	7,867	−70.8	32.1
Connecticut	(S)	70,423	175,940	149.8	26,297	−62.7	33.4
	(H)	7,830	175,940	840.1	26,297	−97.8	33.4
Delaware	(S)	26,253	70,000	167.2	4,177	−84.1	22.0
	(H)	12,751	58,228	356.6	1,643	−87.1	18.5
Florida	(S)	131,881	935,047	617.6	9,543	−92.7	12.0
	(H)	36,951	935,047	498.0	19,543	−94.5	12.0
Georgia	(S)	73,022	556,326	661.9	13,050	−82.1	22.6
	(H)	14,666	556,326	864.0	13,505	−90.2	22.6
Hawaii	(S)	22,567	14,796	83.1	3,397	−58.0	23.4
	(H)	11,687	4,796	18.1	2,257	−43.0	47.8
Idaho	(S)	15,163	93,460	516.4	915	−94.0	16.6
	(H)	9,578	15,576	47.1	915	−91.4	32.7
Illinois	(S)	173,810	565,300	225.2	53,500	−69.2	28.7
	(H)	56,872	160,200	181.3	34,433	−39.6	39.9

* "Minimum Majority": Minimum Majority figures indicate the smallest percentage of a state's population that could elect a majority in each legislative house. The lower the percentage, the less representative of population is the apportionment. For example, in Nevada only 8 percent of the state's voters could have elected a majority bloc in the Senate.

State Units		Population Mean	Most Populous District	% Over State Average	Least Populous District	% Under	"Min* Maj"
Indiana	(S)	111,758	171,089	83.5	39,011	−58.2	40.4
	(H)	65,963	79,538	70.6	14,804	−68.2	34.8
Iowa	(S)	55,149	266,314	383.2	29,696	−46.1	35.2
	(H)	22,676	133,157	421.5	7,910	−69.0	26.9
Kansas	(S)	54,446	343,231	530.2	16,083	−70.5	26.8
	(H)	17,954	68,646	293.9	2,069	−88.1	18.5
Kentucky	(S)	80,077	131,906	65.0	45,122	−43.6	42.0
	(H)	30,373	67,789	123.1	11,364	−62.6	34.1
Louisiana	(S)	83,058	248,427	197.5	31,175	−62.7	33.0
	(H)	29,446	120,205	287.5	6,909	−77.7	34.1
Maine	(S)	26,211	45,687	60.3	16,146	−43.4	46.9
	(H)	5,955	13,102	104.1	2,394	−62.7	39.7
Maryland	(S)	107,030	492,428	360.6	15,481	−85.5	14.2
	(H)	21,232	82,071	180.2	6,541	−77.7	25.3
Massachusetts	(S)	127,405	199,107	54.7	86,355	−32.9	44.6
	(H)	21,825	49,478	130.6	3,559	−83.4	45.3
Michigan	(S)	230,118	690,259	244.0	55,806	−72.2	29.0
	(H)	73,968	135,268	90.2	34,006	−52.2	44.0
Minnesota	(S)	51,370	99,446	95.2	26,458	−48.1	40.1
	(H)	26,763	99,446	281.6	8,343	−68.0	34.5
Mississippi	(S)	43,511	126,502	184.6	14,314	−67.8	34.6
	(H)	16,085	59,542	282.7	3,576	−67.0	29.1
Missouri	(S)	126,559	155,683	22.5	96,477	−24.1	47.7
	(H)	27,400	52,970	99.9	3,960	−85.1	20.3
Montana	(S)	21,049	79,016	555.8	894	−92.6	16.1
	(H)	6,183	12,537	60.7	894	−87.6	36.6
Nebraska		32,822	51,757	57.7	18,824	−42.6	36.6
Nevada	(S)	16,104	127,016	656.9	568	−96.6	8.0
	(H)	4,208	12,525	62.4	568	−92.6	35.0
New Hampshire	(S)	25,285	41,457	63.9	15,829	−37.4	45.3
	(H)	1,343	4,330	185.4	3	−99.8	43.9
New Jersey	(S)	288,893	923,545	219.7	48,555	−83.2	19.0
	(H)	106,539	143,913	42.3	48,555	−52.0	46.5
New Mexico	(S)	29,719	262,199	782.3	1,874	−93.7	14.0
	(H)	11,083	29,133	102.4	1,874	−87.0	27.0
New York	(S)	280,014	425,276	47.8	190,343	−33.8	36.9
	(H)	108,272	190,343	70.1	14,874	−86.6	38.2

State Units		Population Mean	Most Populous District	% Over State Average	Least Populous District	% Under	"Min* Maj"
N. Carolina	(S)	99,009	272,111	198.6	45,031	−50.6	36.9
	(H)	34,610	82,059	116.1	4,520	−88.1	27.1
N. Dakota	(S)	12,877	42,041	225.7	4,698	−63.6	31.9
	(H)	5,898	8,408	52.9	2,665	−51.5	40.2
Ohio	(S)	266,788	439,000	52.4	228,000	−20.9	41.0
	(H)	54,077	97,064	37.0	10,274	−85.5	30.3
Oklahoma	(S)	50,946	346,038	553.9	13,125	−75.2	24.5
	(H)	14,780	62,787	226.6	4,496	−76.8	29.4
Oregon	(S)	53,425	69,634	18.1	29,917	−49.3	47.8
	(H)	27,716	39,660	34.5	18,955	−35.7	48.1
Pennsylvania	(S)	226,380	553,154	144.3	51,793	−77.1	33.1
	(H)	51,210	139,293	158.4	4,485	−91.7	37.7
Rhode Island	(S)	19,299	47,080	152.0	486	−97.4	18.1
	(H)	8,331	18,977	120.8	486	−94.4	46.5
S. Carolina	(S)	51,790	216,382	317.8	8,629	−83.4	23.3
	(H)	18,164	29,490	53.5	8,629	−55.1	46.0
S. Dakota	(S)	18,793	43,287	122.6	10,039	−48.4	38.3
	(H)	8,833	16,688	83.9	3,531	−61.1	38.5
Tennessee	(S)	120,530	237,905	120.1	39,727	−63.2	26.9
	(H)	35,449	79,301	120.1	3,454	−90.4	28.7
Texas	(S)	308,531	1,243,158	302.3	147,454	−52.3	30.3
	(H)	55,262	105,725	68.2	33,987	−45.9	38.6
Utah	(S)	25,704	64,760	81.8	9,408	−73.6	21.3
	(H)	9,122	32,380	132.7	1,164	−91.6	33.3
Vermont	(S)	12,033	18,606	43.2	2,927	−77.5	47.0
	(H)	1,585	33,155	1,991.8	38	−97.6	11.6
Virginia	(S)	99,383	385,194	187.6	51,637	−47.9	37.7
	(H)	39,978	142,597	259.5	20,071	−47.4	36.6
Washington	(S)	57,636	145,180	149.3	20,023	−65.6	33.9
	(H)	28,362	57,648	100.0	12,399	−57.0	35.3
W. Virginia	(S)	58,138	252,925	117.5	74,384	−36.0	16.7
	(H)	17,482	252,925	1,259.5	4,391	−76.4	40.0
Wisconsin	(S)	119,690	208,343	73.9	74,293	−38.0	45.0
	(H)	39,529	87,486	121.3	19,651	−50.3	40.0
Wyoming	(S)	11,142	30,074	146.0	3,062	−75.0	26.9
	(H)	5,439	10,024	70.1	2,930	−50.3	35.8

influence—remained in the hands of the political party or faction that was stronger in the smaller towns and rural areas.[8]

Urban self-consciousness, political awareness, and consequent demands for a greater share of political power developed most strongly during the years 1900–1930.[9] The primary obstacle facing these class-oriented urban interests seeking to alter the state's prevailing power structure was the absurdity of attempting to change it with votes.

The political system seemed to insure the special interests of continued political monopolization by safely embedding them in the political process through the representation formula. By structuring the institutions and organization of government, whose primary function is the channeling of conflict, local/rural interests were able to block access to the political system for more than half a century.[10] As Justice Tom C. Clark, of the United States Supreme Court, said in his 1962 concurring opinion—in the watershed case, *Baker v. Carr:*[11]

> The majority of the people of Tennessee have no "practical opportunities for exerting their political weight at the polls" to correct the "existing invidious discrimination." The state has no initiative and referendum (nor has it other practical opportunities) present under the law. The majority of the voters have been caught up in a legislative strait-jacket. Tennessee has an "informed, civically militant electorate," and "an aroused popular conscience," but it does not sear "the conscience of the people's representatives." This is because the legislative policy has riveted the present seats in the Assembly to their respective constituencies, and by the votes of their incumbents a reapportionment of any kind is prevented. The people have been rebuffed by the Assembly; they have tried the constitutional convention route, but

since the call must originate in the Assembly it, too, has been fruitless. They have tried the Tennessee courts with the same result, and Governors have fought the tide only to flounder. It is said that there is recourse in Congress and perhaps that may be, but from a practical standpoint this is without substance. To date Congress has never undertaken such a task in any state.

Faced with this situation, in 1962 the Supreme Court cautiously involved itself in the "political thicket" of the apportionment issue. As Clark said, "we therefore conclude that the people are stymied and, without judicial intervention, will be saddled with the present discrimination in the affairs of their state government."[12] In involving itself into this controversial and politically crucial issue, the Supreme Court judges have become defenders of particular theories of democracy and have attempted to resolve the controversy on the basis of their commitment to these particular theories. The Chapters in this portion of the study will deal with these opinions; the theories and the empirical and legislative dimensions are included in these Chapters that follow as well as evaluations of these concepts and actions of the judges.

c. The Effects of Malapportionment

Before discussing Supreme Court involvement in this issue, however, one important manifestation of the apportionment controversy must be mentioned: the effect of malapportionment. "The final and crucial question on apportionment," wrote Duane Lockhard, "must be: What does it matter? What ultimate difference does it make that the rural small-town element, heterogeneous, is over-represented in most states?"[13]

Some political scientists believe that malapportionment is not a significant political variable which accounts for particular public policy choices or particular party structures. "On the whole, policy choices of malapportioned legislatures are not noticeably different from the policy choices of well-apportioned legislatures."[14] Others, such as Malcolm Jewell, see malapportionment in a different light: "the problem is an inescapable part of the electoral process and has major partisan implications in most states."[15] Gordon Baker, another commentator, sees clearly perceived results of malapportionment in the form of specific public policy differences, political party structure, and of divided control of government.[16]

These scholars indicate that "the only meaningful way to understand the effects of malapportionment is through close analysis of particular states."[17] Political reality is the important measuring rod in determining the effects of malapportionment. While statistics may show malapportionment, such quantification "necessitates a simplification of what may be a very complex question. The consequences of reapportionment may be so subtle and diverse that they defy quantitative measurement."[18] Although this study does not go into the specifics of malapportionment, a perusal of the readings points to a general consensus among political scientists on two or three consequences of malapportioned legislatures: (1) divided control of government, (2) handicaps presented to minority parties and groups in one-party states, and (3) indications that malapportioned legislatures account for variations in public policy outputs in various states.

In discussing these consequences of malapportionment, one must not forget that, contrary to an earlier view that America's problem was that of "making a great city in a few years out of nothing,"[19] the fact is that "the people of the United States have become metropolitan before realizing their change from a rural to an urban population."[20] By 1960, nearly two-thirds (112.9 million people) of the nation's population lived within the 212 Standard Metropolitan Statistical Areas (SMSAs), accounting for 84 percent of all the increases in the total population between 1950 and 1960.[21] The population within these SMSAs has more and more tended to be distributed along economic and racial lines. The central (core) city has become the place of residence of new arrivals in these areas: non-whites, low-income workers, younger couples, the elderly, as well as displaced, uprooted farmers. It has become "a haven, a ghetto, for those groups not wealthy enough or, through restrictive measures, not allowed to settle in the suburbs."[22]

Suburbia, the outer rim of the SMSA, has rapidly become the "Eden" for middle-class families fleeing the core city. In the decade between 1950 and 1960, all 22 cities with populations of 500,000 or more showed an increase in the percentage of non-white population, whereas all but seven of these cities lost between 6.7 to 33.3 percent of their white population.[23]

While these metropolitan regions are statistically uniform, there are many racial, social, political, and economic differences that distinguish the core cities from the suburbs: rapid growth versus decay; social homogeneity versus heterogeneity; public safety problems; congestion, transportation, housing, air pollution, educational facilities. One complexity of malapportionment is that urban, i.e., core city representatives, have frequently opposed legislative reapportionment (and have worked together with rural legislators to deny the suburban legislators' demands for more equitable reapportionments favoring suburbia) .[24]

Therefore, in discussing malapportionment, one must be aware of (1) the great difficulties and complexities in governing, apportioning, and representing these fragmented metropolitan areas, (2) the inadequacy of using the simplistic rural-urban dichotomy in explaining the existing malapportioned legislatures today, and (3) that, while urbanization was the factor that led to intentional malapportionment, due to the growth of the metropolitan area, it is no longer directly related to the controversy.

(1) Divided Control of Government

Studies made of political activity in the state legislatures of Michigan,[25] Connecticut,[26] Iowa,[27] New York[28] and Pennsylvania[29] indicate that malapportioned legislatures do have obvious political consequences in two-party states where rural counties are over-represented in at least one house or where Democratic party strength is heavily concentrated in a state's few metropolitan areas. It has been shown in these studies that malapportionment accounts for divided control of government. As of 1962, many states had "constitutionally Republican" chambers due to malapportionment, which lead to divided control between the Executive and Legislative branches.[30]

Divided control is accompanied by a diminution of legislative cohesion,[31] political stalemate and irresponsibility (passing the buck) in Michigan and Connecticut, New York and Iowa. And legislative chambers that are closely divided because the losing party—usually the Republican party—due to malapportionment is able to control and win in the over-represented rural counties. The consequence: frustration of the winning party's attempts to carry through legislative programs or depriving the winning party of a strong, cohesion-producing majority. In 1959, in Pennsylvania, such "skewed representation of this sort deprived the Democrats of a badly needed working majority."[37]

(2) Handicaps in One-Party States

Studies indicate that in one-party states in the South, an emerging minority party can be handicapped "because a popularly elected governor of that party may be unable to make an impressive record if the legislature is controlled (sometimes overwhelmingly) by the opposition."[33] Republican party strength is at a disadvantage in the South; where it does exist, the party faces the inequities of malapportionment somewhat analogous to that faced by suburban centers of power in northern states.

Maryland, for example, had a Republican governor, Theodore Roosevelt McKelden, from 1951–1958, but he was faced with a solidly Democratic legislature throughout every one of his years in office. As was written:[34]

> The basic arithmetic of Maryland politics in that the Republican centers (Baltimore city, Montgomery, Baltimore, Prince Georges and Anne Arundel counties) have 76 per cent of the state's population but only 34 per cent of its Senators and 49 per cent of its delegates. The remaining 19 counties, with about 24 per cent of the population, have 68 per cent of the Senators and 51 per cent of the delegates. Thus, while most Marylanders are industrial, white collar, or government workers living in metropolitan areas, political power in the state is held by fishermen, truck farmers, and tobacco growers who are unsympathetic to urban needs.

Malapportionment has its racial consequences in the

South. The 1961 Commission on Civil Rights Report on Voting pointed out that the political weight of an area (consisting of Negroes and other minorities) is less, proportionately, than that of other comparable areas where there are few or no Negro voters. Outright discrimination itself, the Report indicated (by preventing Negroes from voting), produces or exaggerates the malapportionment.[35]

Louisiana (see Table III), Alabama, and Mississippi are southern states that exhibit these consequences of malapportionment and discrimination. There is a serious

TABLE III

Proportionate Representation in Selected Louisiana Parishes, 1960

(1) Parish & Character[1]	(2) Population	(3) Number of Rep's.	(4)	(5) Proportionate Representation	(6) Voting Age Whites Registered	(7) Voting Age Non-Whites Registered	(8) Non-White Population	(9) Adjusted Proportionate Representation[2]
RURAL					—Per Cent—			
Acadia	49,931	2		1/25,000	89.0	82.9	9,827	1/25,000
Madison	16,444	1		1/16,000	81.4	0.0	10,677	1/6,000
Red River	9,978	1		1/10,000	104.4	1.2	4,746	1/5,000
St. Helena	9,162	1		1/9,000	104.9	59.7	5,086	1/9,000
URBAN								
Calcasieu	145,475	2		1/73,000	69.1	49.3	30,375	1/73,000
Jefferson	208,769	4		1/52,000	79.4	57.2	31,924	1/52,000

1. Urban or rural characterization depends upon presence in parish of a city of over 100,000 population.

2. Adjusted by subtracting nonwhites (Col. 8) from total population where insignificant registration of nonwhites (Col. 7) implies racial disenfranchisement.

SOURCE: United States Commission on Civil Rights Report Number One, *Voting*, 1961, p. 115.

malapportionment in the selected parishes in terms of total population ratios and urban-rural makeup. There is also present an "apparent disenfranchisement" of nonwhites in the rural, northern parishes of Madison and Red River. Finally, there is an intensified disproportion created by this racial disenfranchisement.

(3) Effect of Malapportionment on Public Policy-Outputs

"What does it matter?" was the question that opened up this discussion of the effects of malapportionment. Pinpointing malapportionment as *the* intervening variable that accounts for the presence or absence of a certain form of public policy output is a most difficult task.[36]

> For one thing, influences on the legislative product are myriad, and variables differ in relative importance from state to state. It appears that the apportionment structure has been highly significant in affecting policy outcomes in some states, while in others it has only a slight or negligible bearing, at least on *positive* enactments of public policy.

In answering the question what is the difference, political scientists believe that the key is the "minority's potential-nay-saying power—not the likelihood that such groups will constitute a cohesive and continuous bloc."[37] New Jersey,[38] Illinois,[39] Maryland,[40] New York,[41] and California[42] politics offer examples in recent years where positive enactments were denied by legislative minorities and where, because the legislative system "was based upon an unequal allocation of popular strength," "special advantages" were received by certain interest groups.[43] While a significant correlation between public policy output and malapportionment cannot be drawn at this time,[44] it is important to note that, in certain settings, a malapportioned legislature, by simply not acting on crucial issues, can vitally affect public policy-making.

d. Malapportionment and a Commitment to Democracy

"Where there is competition there is a possibility for improvement," wrote Duane Lockhard, "for the simple reason that the ins are opposed by the outs and each tries to turn to its advantage any indiscretion of the other."[45] Malapportionment cuts down the possibility of improvement on principle; it negates or denies the possibility of social change and experimentation by denying or blocking access of certain interests from actively participating in the political process.

If "political equality" is to be an empirically realizable instrumental norm in modern, mass, mobile society, the political process and the system must be kept open to all interested sub-groups. Malapportionment, (1) because it does seem to account for a restriction of conflict and of competition in the political process, (2) because it blocks "effective majority rule or, conversely, responsiveness of the power centers to major constituencies," as well as (3) "the extent and quality of techniques available to out-of-power groups for communicating new facts and ideas to the existing majorities or power-wielders,"[46] even if there are no significant correlations backing up the view, is antithetical to the logic of democracy. Democracy presupposes experimentation and fallibility; malapportionment—signifying the *status quo anti* (*population shifts*) — would seem to deny these characteristics.

Even if the public policy outputs of a well-apportioned state are similar to the public policy outputs of a similar-though-malapportioned state, given a commitment to the logic of democracy and the fundamental principles of that theory that have been outlined in the preceding chapter, the latter legislative assembly (ies) violates the principle of democracy. If there is a *prima facie* case of malapportionment existing in a particular state, the state Constitution allowing minority control of the political machinery or the state legislature deliberately ignoring the commands of the state Constitution, standards of political and legal behavior call for a redress of grievances. In the apportionment issue, as in other issues that have come before it, because of inaction on the part of other branches of government—coordinate and subordinate—the Supreme Court became involved. The remainder of this chapter deals with the first major contemporary apportionment case to come before the Court, *Colegrove v. Green,* in 1946.

I. COLEGROVE V. GREEN: THE CONTEMPORARY SUPREME COURT'S INITIAL RESPONSE TO THE ISSUE

Schattschneider once wrote that when "private conflicts are taken into the public arena it is precisely because someone wants to make certain that the power ratio among the private interests most immediately involved shall not prevail."[47] In a similar vein, Daniel Elezar wrote that "when a problem emerges as a public concern in the United States it has emerged as a concern of publics at all levels of government, in the states and localities as well as in the nation as a whole."[48] In the Negro rights struggle these statements were true; so, too, in the apportionment conflict. And as in the early Negro rights cases there were setbacks, so too in the apportionment issue. *Colegrove v. Green,* decided in 1946, was to be the decisive determinant for over a decade in denying remedies for those citizens who claimed deprivation of civil rights. What follows is a brief view of the decision and an evaluation of the opinions presented by the judges.

In 1946, Kenneth Colegrove, a political scientist at Northwestern University, and two associates (Peter Chamales and Kenneth Sears), filed suit as three qualified voters in Illinois congressional districts challenging the districting of U.S. House seats in the state. Since the Illinois legislature had failed, since 1901, to redistrict, the populations of these districts ranged disproportionately from 112,116 to 914,053 (based on the 1940 census). Claiming that they were denied the equal protection of the laws in relation to voters in other congressional districts in the state (Colegrove was a member of the seventh congressional district, one of over 900,000 citizens), suit was brought in a Federal District Court in Illinois, under the Federal Declaratory Judgment Act of 1934, to restrain, as officers of the State, the Governor, the Secretary of State, and the Auditor of the State from taking steps to hold the congressional elections in November of 1946.

As indicated, their suit was based on the allegation that the 1901 state apportionment act violated the 14th Amendment "since their vote is much less effective than the vote of those living in a district which under the 1901 Act is also allowed to choose one congressman, though its population is sometimes only one-ninth that of the heavily populated districts."[49] Colegrove contended that this reduction in the effectiveness of his vote was the result of a willful legislative discrimination against him and thus amounted to a denial of the equal protection of the laws guaranteed by the Constitution.

He also claimed that such inaction and subsequent reduction of the effectiveness of his vote violated the "privileges and immunities" clause of the 14th Amendment and Article I "which guarantees that each citizen eligible to vote has the right to have his vote counted when voting for a congressman . . . Colegrove contending that his vote is abridged unless that vote is given approximately equal weight to that of other citizens."[50] The Federal District Court dismissed Colegrove's complaint and he then appealed to the Supreme Court. The fundamental question he was raising was "whether the diminished value of individual votes in densely populated districts today, as a result of archaic apportionment, discriminated against the voters in such a manner as to deny them the 'equal protection of the laws' guaranteed by the fourteenth amendment."[51]

a. The Frankfurter Opinion

Justice Felix Frankfurter announced the judgment of the Court. Because (1) a Federal Reapportionment Act of 1929 had no requirements as to "compactness, contiguity, and equality in population of districts," and (2) for "want of equity," Frankfurter affirmed the action of the District Court dismissing the Colegrove appeal. "We are of the opinion," said Frankfurter, "that the appellants ask of this Court what is beyond its competence to grant. . . ."[52]

In effect this is an appeal to the federal courts to reconstruct the electoral process of Illinois in order that it may be adequately represented in the councils of the Nation. Because the Illinois legislature has failed to revise its congressional representative districts in order to reflect great changes, during more than a generation, we are asked to do this, as it were, for Illinois . . . to bring Illinois districts more in conformity with the standards of fairness for a representative system.

At best, the opinion went on, the Supreme Court could declare the existing Illinois electoral system invalid. This would mean electing representatives to Congress on an at-large basis. "The last stage," maintained Frankfurter, "may be worse than the first," for this judicial action would defeat "the vital political principle which led Congress . . . to require districting." And what is this principle? It is, Frankfurter said (using the words of Chancellor Kent) , "recommended by the wisdom and justice of giving, as far as possible, the local subdivisions of the people of each state, a due influence in the choice of representatives, so as not to leave the aggregate minority of the people, though approaching perhaps to a majority, to be wholly overpowered by the combined action of the numerical majority, without any voice whatever to the national councils."[53]

"Nothing is clearer," wrote Frankfurter, "than that this controversy concerns matters that bring courts into immediate and active relations with party contests. . . . It is hostile to a democratic system," he said, "to involve the judiciary in the politics of the people. And it is not less pernicious if such judicial intervention in an essentially political contest be dressed up in the abstract phrases of the law." If the evils that the petitioners claim do indeed exist, the Constitution "gives ample power to provide against" them, *excluding* judicial correction. Congress, claimed the judge, has the "exclusive authority" to secure fair representation by the states in the House of Representatives and, in Article I, Section 4, the Constitution left to that House "determination whether states have fulfilled their responsibility." And, should the Congress fail to assume its responsibility, the remedy then "ultimately lies with the people."[54]

Throughout America's history, Frankfurter wrote, "the most glaring disparities have prevailed as to the contours and the population of districts. . . . The remedy for unfairness is to secure State legislatures that will apportion properly, or to invoke the ample powers of Congress." For the courts to sustain the action called for by Colegrove would "cut very deep into the very being of Congress. Courts ought not to enter this political thicket." Since the Constitution "has left the performance of many duties in our governmental scheme to depend on the fidelity of the executive and legislative action and, ultimately, on the vigilance of the people in exercising their political rights,"[55] Frankfurter affirmed the dismissal of the complaint by the lower court.

b. The Rutledge Opinion

Justice Wiley Rutledge concurred in the result of the Court's judgment—the dismissal of the case—but, contrary to Frankfurter's views, maintained that the apportionment issue was justiciable. Rutledge was the deciding voice against Colegrove, but the fundamental constitutional and philosophical question of the Court's role in the apportionment issue was 4 to 3 against the Frankfurter philosophy of judicial abstention. Justice Rutledge chose to avoid a judicial decision in Colegrove because the "gravity of the constitutional questions raised was so great, together with the possibilities for collision with the political departments of the government."[56]

While concurring in the decision, he said "I think, with Mr. Justice Black, that its effect is to rule that this Court has power to afford relief in a case of this type as against the objection that the issues are not justiciable." While assuming justiciability of apportionment cases generally, because Colegrove "is of so delicate a character," Rutledge felt obliged to refuse to handle the complaint for fear that it would lead to a clash with Congress. "I think, therefore, that the cure sought is worse than the disease, and the Court may properly, and should decline to exercise its jurisdiction."[57]

c. The Black Opinion

Mr. Justice Hugo Black, joined by Justices Douglas and Murphy, wrote an opinion that dissented from the views of Frankfurter. It was Black's judgment that (1) the District Court did have jurisdiction, (2) the complaint presented a justiciable case and controversy, (3) appellants had standing to sue. Colegrove's allegations that he had been denied "the full right to vote and equal protection of the laws . . . have not been denied. Under these circumstances, and since there is not adequate legal remedy for depriving a citizen of his right to vote, equity can and should grant relief."[58]

It was very easy to see why the 1901 Illinois Act denied the appellants the equal protection of the laws. "If applied to the next election [the Act] would result in a wholly indefensible discrimination against appellants and all other voters in heavily populated districts. The Equal

Protection clause of the 14th Amendment forbids such discrimination." There would certainly be no question that discrimination existed, explained Black, if an Act expressly gave certain citizens a half vote and others a full one. The "probable effect" of the 1901 Act would be that certain citizens, among them the appellants, would have votes only one-ninth as effective in choosing representatives to congress as the votes of the other citizens. "Such discriminatory legislation seems to me," wrote Black, "exactly the kind that the equal protection clause was intended to prohibit."[59]

Black then contended that the 1901 Act, by reducing the effectiveness of Colegrove's vote, abridged the professor's privilege as a citizen to vote for congressmen, thus violating Article I of the Constitution (which states that congressmen "shall be chosen by the people of the several states"). While the Constitution did not maintain an express provision requiring approximately equal population election districts, Black stated that:[60]

the constitutionally guaranteed right to vote and the right to have one's vote counted clearly imply the policy that state election systems, no matter what their form, should be designed to give approximately equal weight to each vote cast: . . . All groups, classes, and individuals shall to the extent that it is practically feasible be given equal representation in the House of Representatives, which in conjunction with the Senate, writes the laws affecting the life, liberty, and property of all the people.

If a State acts to effectively diminish the citizen's right to vote or diminishes the weight and value of that vote, the policy of equal representation is violated. And, while the policy "does not mean that the courts can or should prescribe the precise methods to be followed by state legislatures and the invalidation of all Acts that do not embody these precise methods," it does mean that state legislatures must make real efforts to bring about approximately equal representation of citizens in Congress. This, stated Black, the Illinois legislature had not done and the "admitted result is that the constitutional policy of equal representation has been defeated. Under these circumstances it is the Court's duty to invalidate the state law."[61]

Black could not agree with the political question argument presented by Frankfurter in denying judicial justiciability. Before the Court was a state law which violated the constitutional rights of citizens to cast effective ballots. While it is true, the opinion stated, that voting is part of elections and that elections are "political," it is a "mere play on words to refer to a controversy such as this as 'political' in the sense that courts have nothing to do with protecting and vindicating the right of a voter to cast an effective ballot."[62]

What is involved in the case, said Black, "is the right to vote guaranteed by the Federal Constitution. It has always been the rule that where a federally protected right has been invaded the federal courts will provide a remedy to rectify the wrong done." While such a provision would mean state-wide elections, possibly an inconvenience, "it does have an element of virtue that the more convenient method does not have—namely, it does not discriminate against some groups to favor others, it gives all the people an equally effective voice in electing their representatives as is essential under a free government, and it is constitutional."[63]

d. An Evaluation of the Opinions

Colegrove's question to the courts was whether his allegedly diminished and diluted vote for a Congressman, due to malapportionment, was a form of discrimination prohibited by the Fourteenth Amendment's Equal Protection clause. But the case raised another basic question that called for a value judgment by the courts: is it the duty of the courts to act to provide a remedy when other branches of government fail to act to alleviate an admittedly inequitable situation? Should the Supreme Court attempt to resolve a national problem which no other branch of government seemed willing or able to resolve—especially when plaintiffs raise what seem to be legitimate constitutional questions? Does the view "a denial of constitutionally protected rights demand judicial protection; our oath and our office require no less of us"[64] prevail? In Colegrove, the minority opinion of Justice Black answered affirmatively; the Court was duty-bound to invalidate the Illinois Act because it violated the Constitution. Frankfurter answered negatively. While recognizing the "unfairness" of the situation, Frankfurter's opinion mainmained that the remedy lay elsewhere. In evaluating these opinions, therefore, words must be written that clarify the characteristics of this second question of judicial activities in the social system.

Already indicated has been the simple fact that the Court is not a Nocturnal Council of wise men; they are not saints, nor are they Delphic Oracles isolated from the contradictions and self-deceptions of men. "Since we live on earth, not in heaven, we will always be imperfect . . . whether the decisions were right or wrong, it is the role of the judiciary to make pronouncements" said Justice William O. Douglas.[65] This view of a Supreme Court justice, an "activist" view, maintains the position that changes in constitutional doctrine, due to changes in the makeup of the Court or due to changes in the views of the judges themselves, are not unusual. "Either," continues Douglas, "seems a more honorable, . . . frank course than failure to speak up for the announcement of a constitutional doctrine that the majority disproves."[66]

On the other hand, Justice Frankfurter, in recent times, offered the most articulate judicial expression or philosophy of judicial self-restraint. "It can never be emphasized too much that one's own opinions about the wisdom or evil of a law should be excluded altogether when one is doing one's duty on the bench. . . . The admonition that judicial self-restraint alone limits arbitrary exercise of our authority is relevant every time we are asked to nullify legislation. . . . We are not free to act as a super-legislature," he wrote in 1943. At best, the sole duty of the Supreme Court, its "very narrow function" was to "determine whether within the broad grant of authority vested in legislatures they have exercised a judgment for which reasonable justification can be offered."[67]

Judicial restraint is thus an important factor in these apportionment cases—as in many other issues that come before the Supreme Court. The judge's conception of self-restraint and the extent of its outer limits combined with his oath of office and his commitment to the administration of justice can lead to passionate internal struggles. As Anthony Lewis wrote, after the death of Frankfurter, "much as he strove for disinterest, he remained a passionate man. What took place in his judicial career was really a struggle to control the passions—an effort wiser and more successful in some directions than in others."[68]

As a court of law, Supreme Court justices have sworn an oath to ensure "equal justice under law" to all citizens. In *Cooper v. Aaron*, Chief Justice Earl Warren wrote that "The Constitution created a government dedicated to equal justice under law. The Fourteenth Amendment embodied and emphasized that ideal."[69] In *Colegrove*, plaintiffs raised the basic point that they had been denied the equal protection of the laws. Frankfurter's opinion maintained that the Courts "ought not to enter the political thicket." Black's opinion maintained that if a discrimination exists, "it is the Court's *duty* to invalidate the state law." The former view reiterates the point that the "objective sought" by Frankfurter was continued social respect for the Supreme Court: to enter the "political thicket" would damage the prestige of the Court and, ultimately, weaken it irreparably. The latter view, stating that is the Court's "duty" to enter the controversy, went to the heart of the question raised by Colegrove. In the evaluation of these opinions, the element of restraint cannot be ignored.

Frankfurter's conceptual framework in *Colegrove*, with which he framed the set of phenomena he perceived, was his philosophy of judicial restraint and an implicit commitment not to upset existing political structures even though they may be unfair. Additionally, there is expressed in a footnote a view of representative government that tends to diverge from the "equal representation based on population" idea expressed by Colegrove and Black.

Frankfurter perceived a chaotic situation developing if the Court were to intervene in the issue. A reconstruction of the electoral process by the Courts or the invalidation of the existing electoral system and the subsequent at-large elections of Congressmen (by the Supreme Court) is not an equitable solution, said Frankfurter. He suggested, quixotically, that the people who allegedly claim discrimination bring their complaints to Congress—for the Constitution provides for a redress of such a grievance. If that recourse fails, and if the people cannot "secure state legislatures that will apportion properly," another unrealistic observation of the situation by the justice, then the plaintiffs can find a remedy "ultimately," lying "with the people."

Frankfurter, therefore, because his conceptual framework forces him to deny judicial jurisdiction in this area, presents an inadequate perception of the situation and of the consequences ensuing (or that could ensue) from such a perspective. Empirically, it is quite unrealistic to ask the plaintiffs to secure changes in the apportionment plan from a legislature that had not acted on such requests for over forty years. Nor is it realistic to assume that Congress, which has never acted on the question of a "republican form of government," to act in 1946 (granted that Colegrove and others have the ability to even challenge the constitutionality of the legislative apportionment plan of Illinois or question the legitimacy of the Illinois delegation). And what does "ultimate" recourse to the people of the state mean? Surely, it is unrealistic to suggest that a letter-writing campaign be initiated to force changes in the apportionment plan when apportionment, while politically crucial in the distribution of power, is perhaps the most misunderstood issue of politics insofar as "the people" are concerned.[70]

Frankfurter saw just two choices if the Court granted

the validity of the appellants' claims: judicial reapportionment or at-large elections. He rejected them both on the
grounds that (1) courts should not be involved in the
politics of the people, (2) and that the "last stage" (the
at-large election) "may be worse than the first" (continuance of the malapportionment plan). As to the first objection of Frankfurter, the Courts have always "been involved in the politics of the people,"[71] so that the perceived
consequence Frankfurter shuns is really not alien with
regard to past legal and political customs and tradition.
As for the second, the staging of at-large elections in Illinois, Frankfurter's rejection of this alternative course of
action reflects his fear that a "numerical majority" may
overpower "local subdivisions of the people" so as to deny
the latter "due influence in the choice of representatives."
In this rejection, Frankfurter accepted the simplistic
urban-rural dichotomy that in reality disguises the heterogeneity of the situation. Also, his commitment to the
conceptual framework of "self-restraint" did not allow
him to evidence much fairness and due consideration to
Colegrove's pleas.

Frankfurter's justification for his conclusion lay in his
assertion that the Court "ought not to get into the political thicket." His reasons were the arguments already discussed: chaos, lack of competency, unfair at-large elections,
other remedies available. The reasons presented were not
good ones, in that they did not take into due account the
empirical reality facing Colegrove and others *who had
nowhere to go but to the Courts* for a redress of grievances.
He did not take into account the situational context in
which the *Colegrove* case came to the Courts. (He also,
because of his great concern about continued judicial
respect, denied the empirical evidence clearly showing

that the Supreme Court had been involved in our country's many basic controversial political and social issues since 1789.) His decision was unreasonable because it "advocated and acted upon principles with a degree of conviction out of proportion to their desirability."

The minority opinion, written by Justice Hugo Black, presented another judicial view of the apportionment issue. This view was based on Black's conceptual framework, i.e., a judgment that "state election systems, no matter what their form, should be designed to give approximately equal weight to each vote cast." This commitment framed the justice's perception of the situation faced by Colegrove and others; the "objective sought" by Black was thus to declare a state law invalid if it denies equal protection of the laws, a federally protected right.

Examining the facts in light of the commitment to equal votes, Black found a situation that was untenable given the guarantees and requisites found in the Federal Constitution regarding voting rights and representation. State legislatures must make some effort to bring about approximately equal representation of citizens in Congress. The state of Illinois has not done this, an empirical reality noted by Black, and the "admitted result (based on figures) is that the constitutional policy of equality of representation has been defeated." The voter in certain districts in Illinois has not cast an "effective ballot," and it is the Court's function to "protect and vindicate the right of a voter to cast an effective ballot," Black stated.

While an at-large election might mean inconvenience for some in the state, wrote Black in describing the choice of action he favored, "it does have an element of virtue that the more convenient method does not have—" it gives all the people an equally effective voice. Black, by implication, seems to have accepted the fact that the court was not dealing with a simple and unrealistic rural-urban conflict; that representation via an at-large election is more equitable than representation based on antiquated and unrealistic and constitutionally unjustified apportionment schemes which denied many of the citizens the equal protection of the laws. He does not rule out the possibility and, indeed, the desirability of having "all groups, classes, and individuals . . . to the extent that it is *practically feasible* . . . given equal representation." He maintains, however, that the state has, by its inaction, run afoul of the Fourteenth Amendment's prohibitions against certain forms of state action (or inaction). The reasons presented by Black in his opinion are good ones in that they are based on standards of legal and political rationality. There was a substantive federal question raised; the judiciary did have jurisdiction; the opinion reflected an attempt to narrow the breach between professed goals and ideals of American political theory and the reality of American political events. The opinion was justified because good reasons were presented.

Justice Wiley Rutledge cast the deciding vote in the Colegrove decision. While he agreed with the minority opinion (that the apportionment issue was one that the Court, generally, should discuss on the merits), he believed, based on his perception of reality, that, in *Colegrove*, the Court could not provide a remedy because the time was so short.

So it was that, in 1946, the judgment of the Court (based on a conceptual framework that did not allow the judge to perceive the situation and the consequences of judicial action adequately), unreasonable in nature, denied citizens an outlet—the only one available given inac-

FIGURE THREE

Colegrove v. Green, 328 US 549

Criteria	Frankfurter Opinion	Black Opinion
I. Conceptual Framework		
a. Nature of	"Self-Restraint"; muted commitment to "representation of all local subdivisions of people"	"Equal weight for all votes"
b. "Objective sought"	Continued respect for the Courts	Protection of federally protected rights
c. Definition of the Situation	"Unfairness" may be present, but the remedy lies elsewhere, with Congress, state legislatures, "ultimately," with the people.	Discrimination present, no legal remedy for depriving rights, no action on the part of the state legislature.
d. Adequacy of the definition	Inadequate because it is non-empirical; unrealistic.	Adequate because it asks empirical questions and realistically describes situation.
II. Technical Evaluation		
a. Choices perceived	1. No judicial action-remedy with other branches of government and with the people; 2. Invalidating the electoral process, judicial reapportionment; 3. Invalidating and judicial call for at-large elections.	1. No judicial action; 2. Invalidating plan and calling for at-large elections; 3. judicial reapportionment.

b. Consequences perceived

1. Continued respect for Courts, and action by civically militant populace; 2/3. Bad consequences because Court lacks competence (2), because chaos and greater unfairness would ensue if at-large elections held.

1. Violation of judicial duty to protect federally protected rights, 2. No adverse conditions perceived if at-large election held, 3. Judiciary should not (implies this) apportion.

c. Adequacy

Inadequate because perceived consequences based on non-verifiable assumptions.

Adequate; opinion notes an empirically verified (based on framework) wrong and judges, realistically, that an at-large election is more equitable than continuance of present system.

III. *Terms of the Justification*

a. Good reasons offered?

Good reasons not presented; Courts in the past have entered political controversies; have seen as a duty the protection of federally protected rights; at-large elections are not that unusual and, given standards of democracy, not antithetical, as is malapportionment, to the logic of democracy.

Good reasons offered; narrowing the gap between the standard of political representation (American Democratic theory) and the reality of political representation. Opinion raised the empirical question of who is blocking access and equal representation; answered it adequately.

b. Is there a justification?

An unreasonable one, given the conceptual framework.

A reasonable one, given the conceptual framework.

tion by other branches of government—for a redress of (alleged) grievances. Until 1962, apportionment cases were not heard in state and federal courts: the reason was these denials was the "non-justiciability" of the issue.

The following Chapters deal with cases that, because of changed personnel and heightened awareness of the inequity—certainly philosophically and possibly politically —of malapportioned legislatures, substantially changed the *Colegrove* doctrine. The study of apportionment decisions of the Warren Court begins with what Earl Warren himself considers the most important case decided in his tenure as Chief Justice: *Baker v. Carr.*[72]

NOTES: CHAPTER 2

Introduction:

1. Thorson, *Logic of Democracy,* p. 134.
2. E. E. Schattschneider, *The Semi-Sovereign People,* New York, Holt, Rinehart, and Co., 1960, p. 105.
3. James Wilson, toward the end of the debates, expressed his sentiments on political equality and voting in a general declaration "that would satisfy any gentleman: The majority of the people, wherever found, ought in all questions to govern the minority. . . . If numbers be not a proper guide, why is not some better way pointed out? Numbers were surely the natural and precise measure of representation." In Saul K. Padover, editor, *To Secure These Blessings, The Great Debates of the Constitutional Convention of 1787,* New York, Ridge Press, 1962, pp. 301–302. See also pp. 152–163, 239–249, 271–302. Another observer of the Constitutional Convention, a contemporary observer, points out that the delegates' fear of state malapportionment of Congressional districts produced the clause in section four of Article I "giving Congress ultimate authority to regulate the time, place and manner of congressional elections." Without such a federal power, James Madison said, "the inequality of the representation in the legislatures in the particular states would produce a like inequality in the National Legislature, as it was presumable that the counties having the power in the former case would secure it to

themselves in the latter." Anthony Lewis, "Legislative Apportionment and the Federal Courts," LXXI *Harvard Law Review*, April 1958, pp. 1057–1098, p. 1072.

4. Gordon Baker, *The Reapportionment Revolution*, New York, Random House, Inc., 1965, pp. 14–23, passim.

5. *Ibid.*, p. 27. Table I from *The New Jersey Legislature*. A report submitted by the Eagleton Institute of Politics, Rutgers University, November 15, 1963, to the legislature of the State of New Jersey, pp. 191A–199A.

6. Malcolm Jewell, "Constitutional Provisions for State Legislative Apportionment," *Western Political Quarterly*, June 1955, p. 272.

7. Baker, *op cit.*, p. 27.

8. See Baker, *op cit.*, and Robert McKay, *Reapportionment: The Law and Politics of Equal Representation*, New York, Twentieth Century Fund, 1965, p. 29, ff.

9. John R. Schmidhauser, "Iowa's Campaign for a Constitutional Convention in 1960," Case 30, *Eagleton Institute Cases in Practical Politics*, New York, McGraw-Hill, 1963, pp. 1–4.

10. William Riker, *Democracy in the United States*, New York, Macmillan Co., 1965, p. 61, ff.

11. *Baker v. Carr*, 369 US 186 (1962), at 259.

12. *Ibid.*

13. Duane Lockhard, *The Politics of State and Local Government*, New York, Macmillan Co., 1963, p. 318.

14. Thomas Dye, "Malapportionment and Public Policy," XXVII *Journal of Politics*, August 1964, p. 599; David Derge, "The Lawyer in the Indiana General Assembly," VI *Midwest Journal of Political Science*, February 1962.

15. Malcolm Jewell, *The State Legislature*, New York, Random House, 1962, p. 5.

16. Baker, *op cit.*, Chapter Three, passim.

17. *Ibid.*, p. 146.

18. Dye, *op. cit.*, p. 600.

19. Seth Low, quoted in Richard Hofstadter, *The Age of Reform*, New York, Random House, 1955, p. 175–176.

20. Victor Jones, "American Local Government in a Changing Federalism," II *American Review*, May 1962, p. 3.

21. Bureau of the Census, 1961, figures.

22. Jones, *op cit.*, pp. 8–9.

23. See, *Congressional Quarterly Weekly Review*, "Metropolitan Areas Face Severe Governmental Problems," Vol. XIX, August 25, 1961, p. 1484.

24. Baker, *op cit.*, pp. 57–59.

25. Karl Lamb, "Michigan Legislative Apportionment: Key to Constitutional Change," in Malcolm Jewell, ed., *The Politics of Reapportionment*, New York, Atherton Press, 1962, pp. 267, 269.

26. Lockhard, "Connecticut's Challenge Primary: A Study in Legislative Politics," *Eagleton Institute Cases in Practical Politics*, Case 7, New York, McGraw-Hill, 1960, p. 3.

27. John R. Schmidhauser, "Iowa's Campaign for a Constitutional Convention in 1960," *Eagleton Institute Cases in Practical Politics*, Case 30, New York, McGraw-Hill, 1963, p. 4.

28. Ruth Silva, "Legislative Representation—With Special Reference To New York," XXVII *Law and Contemporary Problems*, Summer 1962, p. 413.

29. Frank Sorauf, *Party and Representation*, New York, Atherton Press, 1963.

30. See, for example, Gus Tyler and David Wells, "New York, Constitutionally Republican," in Jewell, ed., *op cit.*, pp. 221–243.

31. Lockhard, *Connecticut*, p. 26.

32. Sorauf, *op cit.*, p. 22.

33. Jewell, *State Legislature*, p. 30.

34. J. Anthony Lukas, "Barnyard Government in Maryland," *The Reporter*, April 12, 1962, p. 31.

35. United States Commission on Civil Rights, Report No. One, *Voting*, Washington, D.C., 1961, p. 114, ff.

36. Baker, *op cit.*, p. 80.

37. Lockhard, *State and Local Government*, p. 318.

38. See *The New York Times* Accounts, June 29, 1966, p. 34.

39. Lockhard, *State*, p. 210.

40. Lukas, *op cit.*, p. 32.

41. Tyler and Wells, *op cit.*

42. Gus Tyler, "Court versus Legislature," XXVII *Law and Contemporary Problems*, Summer 1962, p. 396, ff.

43. Baker, *op cit.*, p. 48.

44. See, Dye, *op cit.*

45. Lockhard, *State*, p. 210.

46. David Bazelon, *The Paper Economy*, New York, Random House, 1963, p. 400.

47. Schattschneider, *op cit.*, p. 38, ff.

48. Daniel Elazar, *American Federalism: A View From the States*, New York, Thomas Crowell, 1966, p. 23.

49. *Colegrove v. Green*, 328 US 549 (1946), at 567–568.

50. at 568.

51. Allan P. Grimes, *Equality in America*, New York, Oxford University Press, 1964, pp. 89–90.

52. *Colegrove,* at 551–552.
53. at 553.
54. at 554.
55. at 555–556.
56. at 556.
57. at 565–566.
58. at 568–569.
59. at 569.
60. at 570–71; 571–72.
61. at 572.
62. at 573.
63. at 573–574.
64. *Reynolds v. Sims,* 377 US 533 (1964).
65. William O. Douglas, in Cahn, *op cit.,* p. 121-122.
66. *Ibid.,* pp. 144–145.
67. *West Virginia Board of Education v. Barnette,* 319 *US* 624 (1943).
68. Anthony Lewis, "A Passionate Concern," *The New York Times,* February 24, 1965, p. 38.
69. 358 *US* 1 (1958).
70. Mason and Beaney, *op cit.,* p. 323.
71. See C. H. Pritchett, "Equal Protection and the Urban Majority", LVIII, *American Political Science Review,* December 1964, p. 869.
72. Letter from the Chief Justice to the author, dated December 18, 1968.

3

Baker v. Carr

INTRODUCTION

a. The Supreme Court Enters the Issue Affirmatively

If political change is to be brought about through the actions of the judicial branch, the legal strategy of the plaintiffs must clearly indicate that (1) the Courts *could* decide the question, (2) the Courts *should* decide the issue, (3) the decision *would be implemented,* and that, if all else fails, (4) Courts *could fashion* a suitable relief.[1] In Colegrove, three of the judges rejected all four contentions; one, Wiley Rutledge, accepted the first one only; three dissenting justices accepted the four points. Between *Colegrove* and *Baker v. Carr,* the latter case decided in 1962, a series of events weakened the Court's stand on the apportionment issue.

Glendon Schubert has written that there are three functional requisites which must be present in order for the Supreme Court to make major policy innovations: (1) the Supreme Court has to be packed with a majority favoring change in standing doctrine, (2) a national majority favoring such a change must also exist, and (3) the policy change would not jeopardize the Court's capacity to assure success in other policy areas.[2] By 1956, Schubert indicates that with the addition of Brennan to the Court, there was a majority on the Court that favored re-hearing the apportionment issue—but the Court was involved in the racial segregation cases. Judicial strategy called for procrastination, for "one bombshell at a time is enough."[3]

Procrastination, rather than a hasty decision without the forces favoring change gathered together, allowed time for political support to build up. During this time, law review articles and popular journals castigated the evils of malapportionment and the Court's inaction in the face of no alternative courses of action open for urban-dwellers.[4] Also, lower federal courts, in Hawaii[5] and Minnesota,[6] heard apportionment cases on their merits (though because of state and federal legislative reactions, the issues became moot).

Given the nature of national population shifts, national political leaders such as Richard Nixon and John Kennedy, and Republican (Eisenhower) and Democratic (Kennedy) Administrations (which had their Solicitor Generals file *amicus curiae* briefs with the Court on the side of plaintiffs in apportionment cases pending before it) spoke out against the evils of malapportionment.[7] For example, President Kennedy, just a few days after the *Baker* decision, said:

> Quite obviously, the right to fair representation and to have each vote count equally is, it seems to me, basic to the successful operation of a democracy. I would hope that through the normal democratic processes, these changes to insure equality of voting, equality of representation, would be brought about by the responsible groups involved. . . .In [Tennessee] for

many years it was impossible for the people involved to secure adequate relief through the normal political processes. The inequity was built in and therefore there was no chance for a political response to the inequity. . . . .It's the responsibility of the political groups to respond . . . but if no relief is forthcoming, then, of course, it would seem to the administration that the judicial branch must meet a responsibility.

At the time of *Baker,* then, there seemed to be a "latent consensus" in favor of some governmental agency changing the inequity of malapportionment. Robert Mc-Closkey, writing about the case in the *Harvard Law Review,* said that the response to *Baker* was astonishing, that the decisions catalyzed a new political synthesis "that was straining to come into being," and "it may be that most Americans have come to think of some version of the majority principle as at least the presumptive democratic standard."[9]

Thus one could say that in the 1960s, it became "politically feasible" for the Supreme Court, given a Court majority favoring change, and a national majority likely to favor the change (and therefore aid in the implementation aspect of any future decision), to consider raising the issue of malapportionment.[10] At this time, five lawsuits, questioning the apportionment schemes in the states of Tennessee, Michigan, New Jersey, Maryland, and New York,[11] were being initiated. It was the Tennessee case that was used by the Supreme Court to reorient its attitudes toward the issue of reapportionment and, before viewing the opinions written in *Baker v. Carr,* some facts about the conditions in Tennessee must be raised.

b. The Tennessee Case

The Tennessee case was a classic situation, an archetype, of a political development that was common in the United States in 1960. The state had not reapportioned since 1901. Under the Tennessee Constitution, apportionment of both houses of the legislature was to be based on population and reapportionment was to take place every ten years. Since 1901, population shifts in the state made the 1901 Reapportionment Act anachronous. By 1960, House districts ranged from 3454 to 79,301 and Senate districts ranged from 39,727 to 237,905 in population.

All state remedies had been explored by the urban petitioners, but to no avail. They had unsuccessfully asked the state legislature to reapportion itself; they had unsuccessfully asked the state Courts to declare the reapportionment unconstitutional and to have the Courts force the legislature to reapportion; they could not call for a state constitutional convention because such a call had to come from the state legislature and that was impossible considering the legislators' feelings about reapportionment, and Tennessee had no referendum or initiative by which the people might determine the issue. And so the urban petitioners turned to the lower federal courts and, in 1959, initiated a class action in the United States District Court in the middle district of Tennessee.

They asked for a declaration by the District Court that would void, as unconstitutional, the 1901 Tennessee Apportionment Act, and for an injunction that would restrain the defendants from conducting any elections— the next election was a year away—under the 1901 Act. They argued that, by debasing their votes due to the "incorrect, obsolete, and unconstitutional" apportionment, the state was depriving them of their right to "equal protection of the laws" under the Fourteenth Amendment of the Constitution. The 1901 Act, they claimed, disregarded the standard of apportionment described by the state's constitution, "thereby effecting a gross disproportion of representation to voting population, and placed the plaintiffs in a position of constitutionally unjustifiable inequality."[12]

In February of 1960, the special three-man District Court dismissed the case for lack of jurisdiction and nonjusticiability—following the doctrine enunciated in *Colegrove.* The plaintiffs then petitioned the Supreme Court for a "redress of grievances," asking the Court to invalidate the 1901 Act, and as an alternative to have the Court either call for at-large elections or call upon the state to hold an election with equitably apportioned districts, based on the 1960 census.

"The Tennessee citizens felt their cause would be immeasurably strengthened if the Solicitor General (representing the national administration) could be persuaded to enter the case as *amicus curiae* in support of their position. They found a receptive Solicitor General in J. Lee Rankin [who] felt that *Colegrove* was unwise law."[13] (This was a bipartisan move since, when the case finally came before the Supreme Court, the Democratic Solicitor General, Archibald Cox, filed the *amicus* brief.)

Essentially, the brief filed by the Justice Department stressed the following points: (1) that malapportionment is "hostile and capricious discrimination by a State," (2) that citizens have the right to be free of such discrimination and that this right is a federally protected one under the Fourteenth Amendment, for "it has been clear that prohibitions in the Fourteenth Amendment are not confined to discrimination based on color, but extend to arbitrary and capricious action against other groups," (3) that a representation scheme has to be "rooted in reason" but that the Tennessee scheme is not, (4) that the Court does have jurisdiction in this constitutional issue and that "the Court can and should afford citizens important protection of the right to vote under the Fourteenth Amendment by invalidating those discriminations which are so arbitrary and capricious as to lack any rational foundation," (5) that the District Court can and should have granted, after framing, relief, "without overstepping the limits of judicial action," (6) that "if the State legislatures violate the federal Constitution through discriminations against voters, there must be a federal remedy—just as for other constitutional violations," and (7) that the Court could legitimately, following the prescriptions of the Tennessee constitution, redraw district lines: "there is nothing nonjudicial or extra-judicial about such relief."[14]

Wilder Crane[15] and Ben West,[16] commenting on the effects of malapportionment in the state of Tennessee since 1901, point out that one-third of Tennessee's voters (until *Baker*) elected two-thirds of the legislature; that the four metropolitan counties of Tennessee (Shelby-Memphis; Davidson-Nashville; Knoxville; Hamilton-Chattanooga) were the most seriously under-represented; that malapportionment was most striking when one compared the over-represented western portion (stagnant and declining Southern rural area) and the under-represented eastern sector (industrially developing urban area which was loyal to the Union in the Civil War).

Furthermore, legislative proposals condemning Supreme

Court actions in the area of race relations and the refusal of the state legislature to repeal the prohibition against the teaching of evolution and its refusal to allow bars in the counties are actions brought about by the cultural, economic, and geographic malapportionment that discriminates against urban and metropolitan areas. Finally, in viewing, for example, state aid for education and apportionment of the gasoline tax among the counties of Tennessee, inequities exist due to malapportionment in that there is no semblance of "per capita" aid, and that the most under-represented counties were the ones that received the lowest amount of aid in proportion to their needs.

The case was argued before the Supreme Court in the Spring of 1961, again in the Fall of 1961; the Court handed down its decision on March 26, 1962. What follows are the opinions of the Supreme Court and an evaluation of these statements based on the criteria of evaluation discussed in Chapter 1.

I. THE OPINIONS IN BAKER V. CARR

a. The Brennan (Majority) Opinion

For the first time in its history, a majority of Supreme Court justices, in an opinion written by Justice William J. Brennan and concurred in by Chief Justice Earl Warren and Justice Hugo Black (separate concurring opinions were written by Justice William O. Douglas, Tom C. Clark and Potter Stewart), stated that, "if it develops at trial that the facts support the allegations," the debasement of a citizen's vote by action or inaction of a state legislature leading to malapportionment, constituted a deprivation of the "Equal Protection of the Laws" protection provided for by the Fourteenth Amendment of the Federal Constitution, and that such a situation was held to be "a cognizable federal constitutional cause of action."[17]

The normative dimension, the conceptual framework through which the justice defined the situation, indicates that Brennan was committed to these ideas:

1) a citizen has a right to vote "free of arbitrary impairment" by the state[18],
2) that when the citizen's right to vote is impaired, a denial of "equal protection of the laws" may be present, and relief can be sought in a federal court[19], for, quoting from *Marbury v. Madison,* "the very essence of civil liberty certainly consists in the right of every individual to claim the protection of the laws, whenever he receives an injury,"
3) in *Baker,* the citizens are claiming "protection of a political right"[20] to have their votes weighted equally with others in the state,
4) "if discrimination is sufficiently shown, the right to relief under the equal protection clause is not diminished by the fact that the discrimination relates to political rights"[21],
5) Courts "will not stand impotent before an obvious instance of a manifestly unauthorized exercise of power"[22], nor will they promote disorder[23],
6) "judicially manageable standards" under the Equal Protection clause "are well developed and familiar"[24], and,
7) "it is open for the Courts, since the enactment of the Fourteenth Amendment, to determine, if on the particular facts they must, that a discrimination reflects *no* policy, but simply arbitrary and capricious action."[25]

In sum, the normative phase of the opinion, developed in response to a major issue to which "no precedents were available directly on the issue of the meaning of the Fourteenth Amendment in the area of popular representation,"[26] expressed the view that the Courts *could* and *should* act in this area if there was *evidenced* discriminatory state action against individuals because the "Equal protection" clause prohibited it.

Present in this conceptual schema ("sub silentio" as Justice Clark pointed out in his concurring opinion), though not overtly expressed, was a ratification of the argument presented by the petitioners and the Solicitor General, i.e., that state apportionment plans not taking into account the principle of population majorities are discriminatory and violate the (implied) meaning of the "Equal Protection" clause of the Federal Constitution. *How* the Courts were to act, "if the facts support the allegations," was not discussed by Brennan other than to say that there are well-developed and judicially manageable standards available.

The underlying normative assertion in the opinion was that, if the allegations presented by the petitioners were correct, then there was shown discriminatory and capricious action on the part of the state. Brennan was in effect saying—without drawing any standards—that the idea of democracy and of representative government was intimately connected with the idea of majority rule. His normative assertion was that if there was a debasement of the strength of the vote due to malapportionment, this was as antithetical to the idea of democracy as was stuffing election boxes with fraudulent ballots or denying a person the right to vote because of race, sex, or color.

Brennan also emphasized, after "precisely identifying" the issues confronting the Court and "clearly" describing the reasons presented by the District Court for not hearing the case on its merits, that Courts *ought not to be impotent* to correct a violation of the Constitution, while at the same time accepting the allegations of the petitioners as correct.[27] The justice was here implying that if the other agencies of government did not act to "redress a grievance" that was empirically verifiable, the Court was *duty-bound* to do so.

The opinion remanded the case to the District Court; it did not empirically define the substantive situation facing the Court, that is, the question of whether the petitioners' allegations were correct—that it left for the lower Court to examine. The Brennan opinion did, however, say that Courts had jurisdiction, that there was a justiciable cause of action stated "upon which relief can be granted, and that appellants had standing to sue for a redress of grievances in a court of law.

In noting jurisdiction, the Brennan opinion pointed to the Constitutional mandates and the United States Code (28 *USC* 1343 [3] and 42 *USC* 1983) and to an erroneous reading of *Colegrove v. Green*.[28] Also "there was a personal stake in the outcome of the controversy," and the opinion held (quoting from *Colegrove*), "that voters who allege facts showing disadvantage to themselves have standing to sue."[29] The technical evaluation aspect of the opinion, other than commenting on jurisdiction and standing, did not provide for remedies. "It is improper now to consider what remedy would be most appropriate if the appellants prevail at the trial," the opinion stated.[30]

Thus the choices perceived by Brennan were not discussed in the opinion; he did not comment on at-large elections, reapportionment by the judiciary, and therefore he did not note any perceived consequences following upon a judicially applied remedy. (Unless one accepts the implication that the consequence of *any* judicial action—if the facts indicate debasement of voter's rights—would be to strengthen a particular conception of democracy.)

Brennan justified his actions by showing that:

1) "none of the characteristics held to involve a political question are involved here"[31], i.e., "a textually demonstrable constitutional commitment of the issue to a coordinate political department; or a lack of judicially discoverable and manageable standards for resolving it; or the impossibility of deciding without an initial policy determination of a kind clearly for non-judicial discretion; or the impossibility of a court's undertaking independent resolution without expressing lack of respect due coordinate branches of government; or an unusual need for unquestioning adherence to a political decision already made; or the potentiality of embarrassment from multifarious pronouncements by various departments on one question,"[32] and that,

2) *Colegrove v. Green* was mistaken in reading past cases of the Courts, for the Courts do have jurisdiction: "the mere fact that the suit seeks protection of a political right does not mean that it presents a political question,"[33], and that

3) the Court in *Baker* was following the mandates of legal and political standards in that the Federal Constitution, the United Code, and past Supreme Court cases established the fact that the Court had jurisdiction over cases involving the deprivation of political rights.

b. The Douglas (Concurring) Opinion

Justice Douglas's opinion concurred with the majority opinion of Justice Brennan's but went beyond the latter in that it maintained that relief should have been awarded by the Supreme Court. The normative phase of the Douglas opinion expressed a view similar to that of the Brennan conceptual framework. The Justice maintained that:

1) "By reason of the commands of the Constitution, there are several [voting] requirements that a state may not require," i.e., race, color, previous condition of servitude; sex; the "third barrier to a state's freedom in prescribing qualifications of voters . . . is the Equal Protection clause of the Fourteenth amendment."[34]

2) Protection of voting rights is not beyond judicial competence, "judicial cognizance"; "no doubt that the Federal Courts have jurisdiction over controversies concerning voting rights."[35]

3) "It is ludicrous to preclude judicial relief when a mainspring of representative government is impaired. Legislators have no immunity from the Constitution."[36]

4) If the plaintiff's allegations are correct, then "invidious discrimination" is present on the part of the state; the traditional test has been whether a state has made an invidious discrimination. If it has, it has broken the barrier established by the Fourteenth Amendment—it has acted unconstitutionally.[37]

5) "While universal equality is not the test, there is room for weighting;" but the state has weighted the votes of one county more heavily than it weights the vote in another and, if the facts match the allegations, such weighting is not protected by the Constitution.[38]

6) Public officials should carefully observe the Constitution and they should not be so partial "as they commonly are in all elections, which is indeed a

great and growing mischief and tends to the prejudice of the peace of the nation."[39]

In sum, while universal equality is neither the test nor a realistic possibility in apportioning a legislature, Douglas holds to the belief—implicit in this opinion—that democracy is equated with majority rule. In the apportionment issue, the justice's belief is that, while legitimate discrimination may conceivably take place (to protect minorities—another democratic value), the situation in Tennessee was an "invidious discrimination" and that "federal intrusion into the election machinery of the state"[40] was justified in order to redress the grievances of the plaintiffs.

Douglas noted that if the allegations were correct, the situation was an intolerable one and relief should have been granted by the Supreme Court. Court action in favor of the plaintiffs was seen by Douglas as producing a "prophylactic effect" on the Tennessee and other state legislatures.[41] Relief can be accorded "fashioned in the light of well-known principles of equity" and, in a footnote, the Douglas opinion suggests some remedies:[42]

> The District Court need not undertake a complete reapportionment. It might possibly achieve the goal of substantial equality by merely directing respondent to eliminate the egregious injustices. Or its conclusion that reapportionment should be made may in itself stimulate legislative action (as it did in New Jersey and Minnesota).[43]

Douglas justifies his decision by noting that past legal actions have followed similar patterns of "federal intrusion" when obvious instances of state infractions of constitutional prohibitions are presented to the Court. "The legality of claims and conduct is a traditional subject for judicial determination," wrote Douglas in the opinion[44] and, while "adjudication is often perplexing and complicated" and the "constitutional guide is often vague," the judgment of the Court was that the claims presented were legal and fell under the jurisdiction of the Courts. Once this was decided, the Court was duty-bound to decide the issue.

c. The Clark (Concurring) Opinion

The Clark opinion also concurred in that the justice accepted the Brennan view that the Court had jurisdiction. However, the normative dimension of the Clark opinion differed somewhat from the two earlier views presented. Clark's conceptual framework expressed the following ideas:

1) "A patent violation of the Equal Protection Clause has been shown" by the petitioners,[45]
2) "While mathematical equality is not required by the Equal Protection Clause, certainly there must be some rational design to a state's districting. The discrimination here [Tennessee] does not fit any pattern—it is a crazy quilt."[46]
3) Courts will refrain from intervening in the politics of a state "where there is some rational policy behind the state's system."[47]
4) A "rational policy" can be when a state develops a "proper diffusion of political initiative as between its thinly populated counties and those having concentrated masses."[48]
5) "Not believing that numerical equality of representation throughout a state is constitutionally required, I would not apply such a standard albeit a permissive one [a rational one]."[49]
6) The *Baker* decision "supports the proposition . . .

that to be fully conformable to the principle of right, the form of government must be representative. That is the keystone upon which our government was founded and lacking which no republic can survive."[50]

7) Never in the Court's history have the principles of self-restraint and self-discipline "received sanction where the national rights of so many have for so long been clearly infringed."[51]

8) "National respect for the Courts is more enhanced through the forthright enforcement of those rights rather than by rendering them nugatory through the interposition of subterfuges."[52]

Clark's conceptual framework thus stressed the twin ideas of "representativeness" and "rationality." If, upon an examination of the facts which in the *Baker* case clearly indicated the presence of invidious discrimination and, furthermore, there is not evidenced a *rational policy* of apportioning seats, then (in effect) the courts must act to preserve the Republic.

Clark's opinion does not opt for a majoritarian view of democracy: he clearly indicates he would not apply a "numerical standard of representation" and would be perfectly happy with a rational plan that shows a rational "effort to attain political balance between rural and urban populations."[53] So long as the apportionment scheme can be defended as rational by the state, so long as the 1901 statute "represented a rational state policy,"[54] even if urban majorities were under-represented, Clark's normative assertion indicates that he would not rule against such a state policy.

Given his normative dimension, Clark's definition of the Tennessee situation follows. From the record he perceives that 37 percent of the voters elect 20 of the 33

Senators and that 40 percent of the voters elect 63 of the 99 members of the Tennessee House of Representatives. But Clark states that "on its face this may not be invidious discrimination if it can be justified [made rational] by facts."[55] He then notes the facts in the case:

1) The apportionment policy in the Tennessee constitution (statewide numerical equality of representation, with certain minor qualifications) —"which is a rational one."

2) On a county-by-county basis there will be "disparities in representation due to the qualifications" but, as the over-all policy is reasonable, these disparities do not raise constitutional problems.

3) The root of the trouble is not the Constitutional policy of Tennessee; the problem, "the discrimination lies in the action of Tennessee's Assembly in allocating legislative seats to counties or districts created by it. Try as one may, Tennessee's apportionment cannot be made to fit the pattern cut by its constitution."[56]

4) Examination of county and district populations and representation "conclusively reveals that the apportionment picture in Tennessee is a topsy-turvical of gigantic proportions . . . When the entire Table is examined—comparing the voting strength of counties of like population as well as contrasting that of the smaller with the larger counties—it leaves but one conclusion, namely that Tennessee's apportionment is a crazy quilt without rational basis."[57]

5) Discrimination is present among counties of like population:

County	Population	Representativeness
Center	23,000	1.10
Maury	24,000	2.25
Washington	36,000	1.93
Madison	37,000	3.50

Therefore, "the plan is neither consistent nor rational."[58]

6) "If the present reapportionment has a policy at all, it is to maintain the status quo of invidious discrimination at any cost."[59]

In his technical evaluation, Clark notes that the Courts are faced with a situation where, "if there were any other relief available to the people of Tennessee," he "would not consider intervention by this Court into so delicate a field." But Clark insists, contrary to Frankfurter's admonition in *Colegrove* that the people had recourse to Congress, etc., that there are no remedies available to the people other than the Courts.[60] The consequence of Court *inaction* would be continued infringements of the national rights of citizens; the Court's action in the *Baker* case was, in Clark's view, "in the greatest tradition of this Court."[61]

While Clark maintained that Federal courts are not forums for political debates, and should not resolve themselves into state constitutional conventions, legislative assemblies, nor should jurisdiction (this point directed toward Douglas's opinion) be exercised in the hope that such declaration "may have the direct effect of bringing on legislative action and relieving the Courts of the problem of fashioning relief" for "this would be nothing less than blackballing the Assembly in reapportioning the state,"[62] he suggested that "one plan might be to start with the existing Assembly districts, consolidate some of them and award the seats thus released to those counties suffering the most egregious discrimination."[63]

Clark's justification for his proposed plan of action, not accepted by the majority, was that Courts had competence and were duty-bound to act in the face of unreasonable, arbitrary state actions. The Court could not stand by when it had jurisdiction in the area and when there were no other available sources that could provide remedies for the inequities the petitioners alleged existed in the state.

d. The Stewart (Concurring) Opinion

The last of the concurring opinions, Justice Potter Stewart's, was a brief statement that "emphasizes in a few words what the opinion [Brennan's] does and does not say."[64] Maintaining that the Court opinion "decided three things [jurisdiction, justiciability, standing] and no more,"[65] Stewart pointed out that Douglas's, Harlan's and Clark's opinions raised issues that were not pertinent before the Court. The normative dimension presented, briefly, is that "the Equal Protection clause permits the States a wide scope of discretion in enacting laws which affect some groups of citizens differently than others."[66] Indicating only that the Court majority did not reach the merits of the issue, Stewart's opinion, implying a conception of democracy that takes into account area representation, did not contain a technical evaluation. He, evidently, stood by the Brennan opinion's justification for judicial entry into the area of apportionment.

e. The Frankfurter (Dissenting) Opinion

Justice Frankfurter's dissenting opinion reiterated the points he made, and saw accepted for sixteen years by federal and state courts, in the 1946 *Colegrove* opinion. These were (1) that the case did not fall within the jurisdiction of the Courts, it was a "political question,"

(2) that the courts could not provide remedies nor grant relief, and (3) that recourse, if it was to be forthcoming, from the evils of malapportionment must come from a "civically militant public." In *Baker,* Frankfurter's normative views had not changed; they were that:

(with regard to jurisdiction)
1) The majority's disregard of the "inherent limits" of the Court's power "presages the futility of judicial intervention in the essentially political conflict of forces by which the relation between population and representation has time out of mind been and now is determined," and "may well impair the Court's position as the ultimate organ of the 'Supreme Law of the Land' in that vast range of legal problems, often strongly entangled in popular feeling, on which this Court must pronounce."[67]
2) "The Court's authority—possessed of neither the purse nor the sword—ultimately rests on sustained public confidence in its moral sanction. Such feeling must be nourished by the Court's complete detachment, in fact and in appearance, from political entanglements and by abstention from injecting itself into the clash of political forces in political settlements."[68]
3) "To promulgate jurisdiction in the abstract is meaningless." It is devoid of reality for it does not set down what relief, if any, a lower court is capable of affording; the "judges do not have accepted legal standards or criteria or even reliable analogies to draw upon for making judicial judgments.[69]
4) Court ought to stay out of the area because of the difficulty of drawing standards where a "criterion for the allocation of political power would be mere numerical equality among voters," and where there would be problems of finding appropriate modes of relief.[70]

5) The "political question" doctrine is "one of the rules basic to the federal system and this Court's appropriate place within that structure."[71]

6) That the political question doctrine "represents long judicial thought and experience," for, from the beginning of its history, the Court has recognized that there are some issues that do not lend themselves to judicial standards and remedies.[72]

7) There is no clear and explicit constitutional imperative that forces the Court to intervene into matters of state government involving the reapportioning of its legislature.[73]

8) There are no standards of reference available that could be used by the Courts to determine whether or not a vote has been "debased" or diluted. "The Court is really asked to choose among competing theories of political philosophy in order to establish an appropriate frame of government for the state of Tennessee and thereby for all the states of the Union."[74]

(with regard to the question of "representativeness")

9) There is a difference between a denial of the franchise to individuals because of race, color, religion, and sex and the relationships between population and representation that may be challenged.[75]

10) The Court "naturally shrinks from saying that in districting at least substantial equality is a constitutional requirement enforceable by courts."[76]

11) "Room continues to be allowed for weighting. This, of course, implies that geography, economics, urban-rural conflict, and all other non-legal factors which have throughout our history entered into political districting are to some extent not to be ruled out in the undefined vista now opened up by review in the federal courts of state reapportionments."[77]

12) "Apportionment, by its character, is a subject of extraordinary complexity, involving (even after the

fundamental philosophic question is resolved of
who is to be represented in a representative legislature) considerations of geography, demography,
electoral convenience, economic and social cohesive-
ness or divergences among particular local groups,
communications. The practical effects of political
institutions, like the lobby and the city machine,
ancient traditions and ties of settled usage, respect
for proven incumbents of long experience and
senior status, mathematical mechanics, censuses
compiling relevant data, and a host of others."[78]

13) "To put it bluntly, the idea that representation
proportioned to geographic spread of population
is 'universally accepted' as a necessary element of
equality between man and that it must be taken
to be the standard of a political equality prescribed
by the fourteenth amendment, is not true."[79]

The perspective of Frankfurter, garnered above, was
that (1) Federal courts, in the absence of standards, constitutional imperatives, lack jurisdiction and are not omni-
competent advocates who can fashion remedies for such
a manifestly political question, (2) for Federal courts to
involve themselves in such activities would tarnish their
image and would lead to possible weakening of the Court's
"moral sanctions," (3) the standard of "one man, one
value, one vote" was not a realistic one.

Frankfurter's implied conception of democracy and
representative government was that old customs and settled usage—proven over time—were reasonable; that representation can take into account many factors other than
geographic spread of population; and that to espouse the
idea of population equality as the major criterion of representative government is to falsify historical facts.

Using this conceptual framework, Frankfurter saw a

situation that gravely threatened the place of the judiciary in the political scheme of things. He defined the apportionment situation as a blatantly political one and said that "it would be ingenious not to see, or consciously blind to deny, that the real battle is the battle between forces whose influence is disparate among the various organs of government to whom power may be given."[80] He saw that the appellants had the right to vote and to have their votes counted; "they go to the polls, they cast their ballots, they send their representatives to the state councils."[81]

Tennessee has not denied the petitioners the right to vote, he observed, "what Tennessee illustrates is an old and still wide-spread method of representation—representation by local geographic division only in part respective of population—in preference to others, forsooth, more appealing."[82] In short, Frankfurter did not see a situation that presented a clear, unambiguous violation by the state of a constitutional prohibition. Furthermore, he presents an historical picture of the nature of representation in Great Britain, the American Colonies, the States at the time of the adoption of the Fourteenth Amendment, and in Contemporary America, which indicates the "stark fact" that, "if there is any one generally prevailing feature in apportionment practices today, that feature is geographic inequality in relation to the population standard."[83]

Frankfurter therefore concludes that, while other forms of representation may be more appealing than "area representation," the way to achieve the change in standards used by the states to reapportion is to appeal "to an informed, civically militant electorate. In a democratic society like ours, relief must come through an aroused popular conscience that sears the conscience of the people's representatives."[84] Relief should not come from the Courts.

With this definition of the set of phenomena facing the Court, the range of choice was limited. Either the Court could enter an area where it should not be, or the Court should not enter the political arena. Frankfurter, given his normative perspective, chose the latter alternative. His justification: past history indicated that area representation was a dominant feature in legislative reapportionment, and that Courts are not competent enough—dispassionate enough—to involve themselves "with the broad issues of political organization historically committed to other institutions."[85]

f. The Harlan (Dissenting) Opinion

Justice Harlan's dissenting opinion reflected a view of democracy and of representativeness that was similar to Justice Frankfurter's and certainly more explicit than the latter's views. Harlan's conceptual framework exhibits the following ideas:

1) The Equal Protection clause does not support the view that "state legislatures should be structured as to reflect with approximate equality the voice of every voter."[86]

2) "It is surely beyond doubt that those who have the responsibility for devising a system of representation may permissibly consider that factors other than basic numbers should be taken into account."[87]

3) There is a multitude of legitimate legislative policies, along with the circumstances of geography and demography, which could account for the seeming electoral disparities among the counties in Tennessee, for example, the size of the county, the loca-

tion within a county of some major industry which may be thought to call for a dilution of voting strength, economic factors, political factors.[88]

4) "There is nothing in the Federal Constitution to prevent a state not acting irrationally from choosing any electoral legislative structure it thinks best suited to the interests, temper, and customs of its people."[89]

5) The distribution of seats on the basis of area representation "is certainly no less a rational decision of policy than its choice to levy a tax on property rather than a tax on income. Both are legislative judgments entitled to equal respect from this Court."[90]

6) "Rigidity of an apportionment (the deliberate maintenance of the *status quo*) pattern may be as much a legislative policy decision as is a provision for periodic apportionment. In the interest of stability, a state may write into its fundamental law a permanent distribution of legislators."[91]

7) The rationality of the Tennessee legislature is clear: "To preserve the electoral strength of the rural interests notwithstanding shifts in population."[92]

8) The inequality seen in the Tennessee apportionment picture is not based on an "impermissible standard" and therefore, there is no call for a holding of constitutionality of the state policy.[93]

9) "I would hardly think it unconstitutional if a state legislature's expressed reason for establishing or maintaining an electoral imbalance between its rural and urban population were to protect the state's agriculture interests from the sheer weight of numbers of those residing in its cities."[94]

10) The Tennessee apportionment is rational, not capricious, even if it were shown that legislators "had been activated by self-interest in perpetuating their own political offices or by other unworthy or im-

proper motives. It is not the business of the federal courts to inquire into the personal motives of legislators."[95]

Harlan's normative assertions about the nature of representation are clear and unambiguous. Democracy does not demand numerical equality as a standard of political representation; so long as there is a policy presented by the legislature, albeit a discriminatory one against certain types of citizens in the state, the Court ought not to judge the policy.

"Courts cannot decide at what point a valid apportionment plan becomes void—because the factors entering into such a decision are basically matters appropriate only for legislative judgment."[96] State legislatures, he maintained, "should determine what constitutes a balance of representation between geographic and demographic variables."[97]

The definition of the situation, given the sharply delineated conceptual framework, was also clear and precise. "Appellant's allegations, accepting all of them as true, do not . . . show an infringement by Tennessee of any rights assured by the Fourteenth Amendment."[98] Given the normative commitments presented above, the opinion rejects appellant's claims that the Equal Protection clause requires approximate equal voting weight, that "time" has rendered the 1901 Act obsolete "to the point where its continuance becomes vulnerable under the Fourteenth Amendment,"[99] and that there was no capriciousness shown by the state policy.

Harlan's choice of action was to affirm the lower federal court's action dismissing the appeal. That the majority opinion remanded the case to the lower court for further action Harlan saw with misgivings.

Those observers of the Court who see it primarily as the last refuge for the correction of all inequality or injustice, no matter what its nature or source, will no doubt applaud this decision and its break with the past. Those who consider that continuing national respect for the Court's authority depends in large measure upon its wise exercise of self-restraint and discipline in constitutional adjudication, will view the decision with deep concern.[100]

He justified his view that the Courts ought not to intervene by stressing the competency of the legislators to develop apportionment policies—"the product of legislative give-and-take and of compromise among policies that often conflict"—and by indicating that Courts were not competent to hear the case and that there were no constitutional mandates that placed the apportionment controversy in the courts in the first place.

II. THE EVALUATION OF THE OPINIONS

Professor Paul Kauper wrote that in the apportionment case, "in the name of 'equal protection,' the Court majority was in effect opening up the question of what constitutes a republican form of government for judicial examination."[101] The central issue in the apportionment cases, granting the Court's jurisdiction and its ability to provide relief under the Constitution (two equally important antecedent questions that were directly answered by the Court majority in *Baker*), was to be: just what form of apportionment is compatible with a representative form of government, that is, when is an apportionment plan a "fair" one in that it "represents" all interests fairly?

a. Conceptual Frameworks and Definitions of the Situation

In the *Baker* opinions, though the major question was jurisdiction and justiciability, there were—implicitly and explicitly—in the course of commenting on the major question various normative commitments to ideals of representative government. Two broad themes were presented in the six opinions: (1) *majoritarianism* (in the Douglas and, by implication, the Brennan opinions) and (2) a *limited pluralism* which limits the representativeness of "concentrated masses" in urban areas (the Clark, Stewart, Frankfurter, and Harlan Opinions). In the former view, a "fair representation" has to initially and primarily take into account population, although weighting (in the abstract) is not *per se* unconstitutional and mathematical equality is admitted to be a practical impossibility. The latter views stress non-demographic factors including economics, cultural differences, custom and tradition, rational legislative policies of discrimination, etc.

Comparing these normative assertions with the ideas of democracy and representative government presented in Chapter 1, the *majoritarian* view closely approximates the standard while the *limited pluralism* view differs from it. The majoritarian view, like the standard of democracy, emphasizes majority rule and states that, if the facts bear out the allegations, discriminatory and capricious action exists if a minority blocks a majority or another minority from institutionally and practically sharing in the making of public policy in the state legislatures.

The limited pluralism view diverges from the standard because it emphasizes a belief that can lead to the blocking of inquiry in the social and political processes. It does so by stressing the importance of traditions, custom, old usage, "presumptions of rationality" with respect to legislative inaction on the apportionment issue, and, implicitly, wise legislators—i.e., "respect for proven incumbents of long experience and senior status"—who have all the answers.

Holding these normative views of representative government, the Supreme Court justices, again explicitly or implicitly (the Brennan opinion), had to judge—empirically or not, determined by the questions the judges asked—whether an apportionment plan, Tennessee's, allows for the possibility of representative government or whether the plan has *empirically* blocked access to the political processes in such a manner as to brand the apportionment scheme as capricious and discriminatory.

In defining the situation facing the court, the Douglas and Brennan opinions argued that (if the allegations were correct—a matter for the District Court to decide) because majority representation was inadequate due to an unfair and unconstitutional apportionment plan, the Tennessee condition violated the prohibitions of the Fourteenth Amendment.

Justice Clark, perceiving the set of phenomena in the light of his conceptual framework, stated that the apportionment scheme was null and void but argued this point on the grounds that the discrimination shown by the state was a crazy quilt pattern. Implied in the Clark opinion is the substantive view that if a "rational policy" had been present in the Tennessee apportionment plan, discriminating against cities and towns of over 20,000 population, it would not have been judged unconstitutional.

The Frankfurter and Harlan opinions defined the situation in still another way. Indicating initially that the Court should not get into the "political thicket," both

justices argued against the view that the Court had jurisdiction and that it could afford relief to the plaintiffs in
an apportionment controversy. They feared that the
Court's power, based on moral respect of the people,
would be diminished if the Court entered the fray. The
majority view—that the issue fell under the jurisdiction
of the Court because it involved "political rights" protected by the Constitution and that the Court was duty-
bound to enter the controversy—was rejected by the
two justices, who argued for judicial self-restraint and
discipline.

Only after this initial plea did Frankfurter and Harlan
argue that the Tennessee plan was rational—based on
their conceptual frameworks. For various reasons, mentioned earlier, both judges could find no capricious and
discriminatory action on the part of the legislature of
Tennessee. And so, even granting jurisdiction, the two
justices argued that there was reasonable state action.

How adequate are these definitions of the situation?
The majoritarian views do not really investigate the facts
in this situation, although Justice Douglas, in a footnote,
quotes from a report of the National Institute of Municipal Law Officers pointing out the plight of the urban
and suburban citizens in legislative representation and
of their frustrated attempts to achieve better housing,
education, transportation when faced with a rural
legislature.[102]

The Brennan opinion specifically sends the case to the
lower Court so that the District Court could judge the
validity of the allegations of the plaintiffs. The burden
of the majority opinion was to justify Court jurisdiction
in this area in the first place; definitions of the situation
were to be perceived by the District Court. There is a

hypothetical statement made by Douglas and Brennan, that is, *if* the allegations are correct, *then* there is ample evidence that *no policy exists,* but merely capricious and arbitrary action. As such, on this question of the adequacy of their definitions, no judgment can be made on the Brennan and Douglas opinions.

Justice Clark's perceptions of the situation were based solely on mathematical figures and on the construction of "representativeness" formulas. His judgment, that the apportionment scheme was a "crazy quilt," was not based on his answering the question of who has blocked access to the political process. His basic concern was whether or not there appeared in the case a rational state policy; on viewing the facts, i.e., the figures involving representation in the Tennessee Assembly and Senate, he finds "invidious discrimination" because the discrimination cannot be justified or "made rational" by them.[103] His definition, therefore, does not raise the empirical questions dealing with the political reality of the situation. He does not inquire as to the denial of an individual's political rights; nor does he focus on the political and social effects of malapportionment, i.e., the possibility of blocking particular actions by entrenched legislative minority interests. Because of these reasons, the judgment on the adequacy of Clark's definition of the situation is negative.*

As for the Frankfurter opinion, the comments made about his opinion in *Colegrove* are valid in the *Baker* case. His "anguished judgment,"[104] based on his firm

---

* In an interview with Justice Tom C. Clark on January 17, 1969, in his Supreme Court chambers in Washington, D.C., the Justice clearly indicated that he saw the malapportionment controversy in black-white, non-empirical terms. For example, he kept on insisting that fear of "tyranny of the urban majority" was realistic and that this fear, if legislated against properly, was perfectly constitutional.

commitment to judicial self-restraint, did not raise the question of "what has happened in Tennessee because of malapportionment?" at all. Frankfurter believed that the Court should not have to answer such a political question. But then he (and Harlan, too) maintained that the Courts had to presume rationality and good intentions on the part of the legislators, respecting these political actors' good judgments based on their collective wisdom. Frankfurter does note, in a footnote, that "recent Tennessee legislature's have failed, as did their predecessors, to enact reapportionment legislation, although a number of bills providing for reapportionment have been introduced."[105]

However, he notes this fact *after* stating that "appeal must be to an informed, civically militant electorate. In a democratic society like ours, relief must come through an aroused popular conscience that sears the conscience of the people's representatives."[106] This suggestion of the justice, as will be suggested in the evaluation of Frankfurter's perceived consequences and choices, is not a very realistic one, as Justice Clark pointed out in his concurring opinion.[107] In sum, the Frankfurter opinion does not adequately define the situation because he does not raise the empirical questions.

Frankfurter does not raise these questions because his conceptual framework and his perceptual vision do not permit him to do so. His is the anguished judgment of the jurist who faces a situation where a legislature adopts a statute limiting the right to speak and write of a group of social, political, or economic heretics. "Such a judge might be reluctant to employ judicial review against it. If free expression is limited by a frightened and myopic majority (in apportionment, the "majority" meant the minority of the population of a state), the possibility of changing social goals is blocked to that extent."[108]

Because he denies the primacy of the "representation according to the spread of population" criterion, Frankfurter (1) does not perceive empirical (apportionment) question; (2) accepts the view that no constitutional right was violated in the Tennessee case, and (3) defends his views by presenting an essay in past history of representation in England, the colonies, and the United States—indicating that because the population standard was denied by states in the past, such deviations are legitimate. In terms of the initial hypothesis, the Harlan opinion is also inadequate, but for slightly different reasons. Justice Harlan indicates in a footnote that he is somewhat aware of the empirical situation:[109]

> It is primarily the eastern portion of the state that is complaining of malapportionment, along with the cities of Memphis and Nashville. But the eastern section is where industry is principally located and where population density, even outside the large urban areas, is highest. Consequently, if Tennessee is apportioning in favor of its agricultural interests, as constitutionally it was entitled to do, it would necessarily reduce representation from the east. . . . Surely one need not search far to find rationality in the legislature's continued refusal to recognize the growth of the urban population. . . . The foremost legislative motivation has been to preserve the electoral strength of the rural interests notwithstanding shifts in population.

Harlan is aware of the empirical conditions, *but* he maintains that it is perfectly reasonable for a legislature to block access to the political process of industrial and urban interests and to protect agricultural interests in the legislature. While his perception of the situation may not be classified as inadequate, Harlan's conceptual framework leads him to deny the possibility of blockage in the legislative scheme.

In a sense, Harlan does not raise the empirical question. Like Clark, he views the mathematics as well as the economics of the situation and he determines that there was no irrational action shown. Judging his observations—and his acceptance of obvious inequities—in light of the brief statement of facts presented earlier in the Chapter, one would have to classify his definition of the situation as inadequate.*

b. The Technical Evaluation and the Terms of the Justification Phases

Turning to the technical and justification aspects of the opinions, the Brennan opinion's choices are two. Either the Court was to take no action or it was to take action that would enable Courts to remove arbitrary impairment of citizen's rights under the Constitution. The consequence of the first choice, according to the opinion, was continued denial of constitutionally protected rights (as other branches of state and federal government were not about to act to redress the grievances of the plaintiffs). The consequences foreseen by Brennan if the Court chose the second alternative were constitutionally, and normatively, more agreeable to the justice. For if the Court were to provide the plaintiffs with a channel for the redress

---

* Speaking with Justice Harlan on February 25, 1969, he reinforced his commitment to a pattern of weighted representation for various economic and demographic minorities, regardless of the population inequality that such alignments created or continued to maintain in existence.

of grievances, the gap between democratic theory and democratic practice would be closed.

Brennan's opinion indicated that relevant data was viewed. For example, information was presented in the opinion that showed Brennan's awareness of population shifts[110] and of the impotency of the people to act to redress their grievances.[111] He also presented relevant precedents, Constitutional prescriptions, and United States Statutes[112] that provided the rationale for Court action in the apportionment area.

Due to the nature of the legislative dimension, however, Brennan specifically did not examine the allegations closely; this was to be the task of the Federal District Court. Due consideration was superficially shown in that the state of Tennessee had the opportunity to defend the apportionment scheme in the lower court, i.e., attempt to show that the plan reflected a reasonable state policy. Also, the Brennan opinion did not indicate that mathematical equality was to be the standard (it did not present any standard for use by the lower courts) and indicated, only by implication, that weighting to a certain degree may be permissible—if the majority is equitably represented.

Almost all facets were discussed by Brennan, although the questions of standards, remedies, and the most important question of the nature of "representative government" were not. (It may be that the majority opinion, aware of the fact that precedent was being set by Court involvement in the apportionment controversy, wanted to go slow and feel out the response to Court involvement as well as find out, by thinking out, what "representative government" really meant and then formulate standards and suggest remedies. Tactics and strategy would seemingly suggest that the Court should, very carefully, walking on eggshells, enter the issue.) [113]*

How adequate was the Brennan technical evaluation? Given its commitment to majoritarianism and, implicitly, to open-endedness and fallibilism, as well as its awareness of the empirical inequities that existed in the state of Tennessee, it would seem to be fairly adequate. The basic burden of the evaluation was to indicate Court jurisdiction in this area. In judging the situation facing the plaintiffs, the Brennan opinion summarized that, if the Court did not enter the issue (and Brennan defended the notion that the Court was constitutionally and statutorily duty-bound to enter the fray), nothing would be done to alleviate the alleged injustice. Brennan did not use a crystal ball to reach this judgment; he used instead the history of Tennessee (and other states) since 1901 to defend his assertion. It would seem that his judgment was adequate, given the past history of legislative inaction.

The justification for the Brennan decision must also be judged adequate for the following reasons. First of all, the means used to arrive at the decision were logically consistent, plausible, and clearly presented. Brennan raises and discusses the two pertinent issues (jurisdiction and justiciability) in a reasonable manner. Considering that Brennan had no precedents to use in regard to appor-

---

* In interviews with Justices Tom C. Clark, John M. Harlan, Jr., Hugo Black and William O. Douglas on January 17 and February 25, 1969, there was unanimous opinion (expressed also, in the large [6] number of written opinions) expressed by these Justices that the Court majority (1) did not know the precise direction they wanted to take in the apportionment cases and (2) they wanted state and federal courts beneath them to deal with the question of judicial standards. Justice Clark clearly indicated that the upcoming standard of the court "one man, one vote," a "catch-phrase" coined by Justice Douglas, did not appear once in conference session discussions. Furthermore, Clark went on, no standards were discussed at all.

tionment—he does use the *correct* interpretation of *Cole-grove* to indicate jurisdiction—the opinion presented a clear defense and explication of the decision and of the reasons used to reach the decision. Brennan differentiated between "political rights" and "political questions," which was an important distinction to make; clearly showed that the Court, in his view, had a constitutional and statutory duty to protect the citizen against arbitrary state action that restrains his political rights; that "an unbroken line of precedents . . . sustains the federal courts' jurisdiction of the subject matter of federal constitutional claims of this nature" (Brennan had already pointed out that the rights claimed by the plaintiffs were protected by the Constitution) ;[114] that the plaintiffs had standing to sue; and that Courts could provide remedies.

While the opinion was *unclear* as to standards to be applied and remedies available, this lack of clarity could be taken to indicate the court's commitment to fallibilism and open-endedness. The opinion's unclarity could have indicated (1) Court sensitivity to public opinion and to reaction from other branches of the federal and state governments, as well as (2) uncertainty as to the appropriate standard—although implicit in the opinion is a vague commitment to the idea of majoritarianism. This meant procrastination, during which time the Court was to reexamine the question (philosophical) of standards on the basis of feedback from lower courts, legislators, executive pronouncements, law review articles, editorial commentary, until another set of cases appeared before the Court concerning the question of malapportionment.

A second reason for stating that the justification was adequate were the arguments Brennan presented for his decision. As indicated in Chapter 1, a good reason is one based on standards of political and legal rationality. The Brennan opinion indicated that the Court had to act in this area because the Constitution and the appropriate statutes (as well as past Supreme Court decisions) placed the burden of responding to claims of citizens regarding deprivation of constitutionally protected rights upon the Federal Courts. In declaring jurisdiction, the objective sought by the Brennan opinion was to close the gap between the standards of political and legal rationality professed by our society and the awkward reality found by the judges. On its face, this has to be judged an adequate reason for justifying its decision.

Overall, then, taking into consideration the novelty of the issue being discussed by the Court and the Court's awareness of the possible consequences that would ensue given Court involvement, the Brennan opinion would seem to be (based on the standards discussed in Chapter 1) a reasonable one. It accepts majoritarianism implicitly; it defines the situation—jurisdiction, standing, justiciability—adequately; it makes use of data; it, by its procrastination, indicates an awareness of the situational context; and it adequately justifies its "legislative" action. Generally, it is reasonable because *"sub silentio"* it states that malapportionment, if present in the state, is capricious and arbitrary, and is antithetical to the idea of democracy and representative government.

The Douglas opinion can also be classified as reasonable. It basically follows the Brennan view, although Douglas clearly condemns oppressive weighting and openly defends a majoritarianism that is only implicitly expressed by the majority opinion. His technical evaluation includes the two choices indicated in the Brennan opinion and adds another choice which Douglas felt should have been chosen by the majority: the Supreme Court, to produce a "prophylactic effect" on the Tennessee and other legislatures, should have accorded relief to the plaintiffs instead of remanding the case to the lower court for trial and, possibly, relief. He indicated that consequences following such a choice would probably replicate the New Jersey and Minnesota situations (where legislatures did reapportion after State Courts threatened to act). His justification basically reproduced the Brennan arguments, that is, that "federal intrusion" into the affairs of the states was permissible under the Constitution and under the appropriate United States Codes when the states allegedly violated a proscription of these documents.

The Clark opinion is a more difficult opinion to evaluate. As was already pointed out, his view was that the apportionment plan was irrational because it was a "crazy quilt" and not because it denied plaintiffs representativeness on the basis of the principle of "majoritarianism." The situation was intolerable, he maintained, because the crazy quilt pattern existed and the citizens had no way to alleviate the inequity.

Clark's impressions of the situation leave no doubt that he was not a majoritarian, that he *was* in favor of a *rational* plan that would take into account rural-urban differences (favoring the rural areas), and that his empirical estimate of the difficulties of the plaintiffs was correct. Clark's technical evaluation, based on his mathematical formula, the raw data—i.e., population figures in the Tennessee counties, and the inability of *any* Tennessee citizen (not just the urban plaintiffs) to acquire a remedy via some form of state action—also stated two choices: (1) judicial non-involvement or (2) judicial involvement, including judicial remedies (in the form of consolidating some of the state districts). The adequacy of the technical evaluation, including the perceptions of consequences should the Court not act, is reasonable. And Clark's structure is also clear and consistent, including the plan by which he is able to interpret the representative nature of the districts.

What seem to be inadequate and therefore what makes his judgment unreasonable are Clark's reasons for his decision. As was indicated in the first chapter, a decision may be judged "good," yet be unreasonable (irrational) or non-rational. While Clark's decision generally agrees with the Brennan opinion—i.e., that there is jurisdiction and that there are remedies available to redress the grievances—the reasons offered to justify the decision are based on (1) an inadequate definition of the situation that (2) ties up the basic question of democracy and representation to the concept of *limited* and *narrow pluralism* which (3) ignores the basic question of whether or not a *rational plan* which denies majority rule is antithetical to the concept of democracy. Clark does indeed say that there has been a blocking by the "status quo" interests of legislative reapportionment and that such a blockage is unconstitutional, but the reasons he offers, based on his conceptual framework, lead one to conclude that the decision, compared to the model of democracy presented earlier, is not adequately justified.

The Frankfurter and Harlan dissents are easier to evaluate than the Clark opinion. Frankfurter's possible choices were two. Either the Court handles the issue and jumps into the "political thicket," or the Court abstains from such a "political question" (advising the plaintiffs to appeal to a "civically militant" electorate for a redress of grievances). As he did in the earlier *Colegrove* decision,

Frankfurter chose the second alternative. It was not an adequate one because, to repeat the point, Frankfurter's choice ignored the empirical question of who has blocked the way to inquiry and to subsequent social and economic change.

Justice Clark succinctly condemned as unreasonable and unrealistic the Frankfurter admonition to the people that they "sear the consciences of their elected representatives" in order to seek change. It was an inadequate response because it did not take into consideration the data presented by the plaintiffs showing the inequities and did not fairly treat the complaints of the plaintiffs, but instead brushed aside their complaints as immaterial and trivial. His philosophy of judicial restraint did not allow the Justice to treat the case impartially. He attempts to show, by presenting a history of representation in England and America, that their claims for equal voting power is not an integral value in the Anglo-American political hierarchy. (The history he presents is somewhat at odds with other accounts of the period.) [115]

He attempts to justify his decision (not to intervene in the controversy) by relying on the "political question" doctrine, on Colegrove, and on the general claim that involvement would generally injure the Court's prestige and power. His justification would seem to be inadequate because (1) Colegrove was, once again, interpreted by Frankfurter incorrectly (he maintained that the precedent established in that case did not allow the court jurisdiction in the area of apportionment—which was not correct), (2) the Court has been involved in "political rights" questions, malapportionment has an effect, minimally prospective, on political rights, and therefore malapportionment cases follow a series of past Supreme Court cases involving "political rights" claims (hence Frankfurter was incorrect in not distinguishing between political rights and political questions), and (3) because Frankfurter was so intensely committed to the principle of judicial restraint in this area he was led to actions that ignored the basic question of blockage of legitimate interests and what this blockage means insofar as standards of political rationality were adversely affected by these inactions of legislators.

Overall, then, on the basis of the criteria and the model of democracy established, the Frankfurter opinion, with its (1) historicist conception of democracy, (2) ignoring of the empirical problems, (3) commitment to judicial self-restraint, would have to be judged unreasonable.

The Harlan opinion is also classified as unreasonable, for it too does not adequately perceive the problem as one involving the lack of representation and, as such, a problem that concerns the nature of meaningful representative government in the twentieth century. Given his *limited pluralism* notion, which emphatically denied the principle of majority rule, his technical evaluation was clearcut. The judiciary should not enter the issue because the matter is one for legislative judgment only.

Harlan chose to affirm the lower court's order to dismiss the appeal. His choice was inadequate for the reasons offered in the Frankfurter evaluation. The choice ignored the empirical question and the fact that the legislature was not about to act to redress the grievances of the petitioners. Harlan was aware of the data indicating a discrimination against the industrial and urban interests by the rural interests but *accepted* the discrimination as it reflected the nature and reality of politics.

Harlan's justification for the decision he reached was inadequate because the reason presented, that legislators were competent to develop apportionment policies whereas judges were not, was far from accurate. The reason was irrational because, in defending a view of the judicial process similar to the self-restraint ideas of Frankfurter, a conceptual framework was presented which led to the presentation of reasons for non-action that (1) ignored the reality of the situation, and (2) denied standards of legal and political rationality by emphasizing a conception of democracy and representation that was antithetical to the society's professed standards.

In the examination of the *Baker v. Carr* opinions, the Brennan and Douglas opinions seem to unconsciously employ or implicitly give voice to a "fallibilistic" conception of democracy. Their opinions underline, again—in Brennan's opinion, by implication—a commitment to the idea that democracy presupposes majority rule and participation in the making of public policy, *along with* adequate minority representation. Without such a scheme of governing, the opinions (and the conception of democracy presented in Chapter 1) seem to indicate the absence of fair representation. They maintain that the Court is *duty-bound* to act so as to allow the social and political systems to leave the way open for change in the making, remaking, and elimination of public policies that have been found wanting. Both opinions, therefore, implied a judicial commitment to experimentation and innovation in governing. The Clark, Frankfurter, and Harlan opinions, because of a commitment to a different conceptual framework, did not see blockage—or did not even raise the question of whether blockage existed at all.

In *Baker*, the watershed case, four of the justices responded to the set of phenomena with a conceptual framework reflecting fallibilism. Because of *judicial cau-*

FIGURE FOUR

Baker v. Carr, 369 US 186

Criteria	Brennan Opinion
I. Conceptual Framework	
a. Nature of the Commitment.	"Majoritarianism" (implicit)
b. Objective Sought	Protection of political rights of the citizen
c. Adequacy of the definition of the situation	*No judgment.* Opinion did not define the situation. Dealt only with jurisdiction.
II. Technical Evaluation	
a. Choices Perceived	1. Deny jurisdiction; 2. accept jurisdiction and remand to lower court
b. Consequences Perceived	1. Continuation of egregious conditions of inequity; 2. relief provided by Courts in absence of legislative action
c. Adequacy of a. and b.	*Adequate.* Data presented; fairness shown; fallibilism indicated.
d. Structure of the opinion	Logically consistent, plausible
III. Terms of the Justification	
a. Good reasons offered?	*Yes.*
b. Is there a justification?	*Yes.* Standards of Political and Legal Rationality followed by opinion
IV. Overall Evaluation of the Opinion	*Reasonable.* Conception of Democracy indicates a commitment to the principle of fallibilism and open-endedness in public policymaking in a democracy.

Douglas Opinion

Criteria

I. *Conceptual Framework*

    a. Nature of the Commitment.   "Majoritarianism"

    b. Objective Sought   Protection of political rights of the citizen.

    c. Adequacy of the definition of the situation   *No judgment.* Situation defined only hypothetically; opinion concurred with Brennan view that issue was justiciable but felt that Court should have provided remedy.

II. *Technical Evaluation*

    a. Choices Perceived   1. Deny jurisdiction; 2. accept and provide relief.

    b. Consequences Perceived   1. Continuation of unconstitutional inequity; 2. force legislatures to respond to demands to reapportion.

    c. Adequacy of a. and b.   *Adequate.*

    d. Structure of the opinion   Plausible, logically consistent.

III. *Terms of the Justification*

    a. Good reasons offered?   *Yes.*

    b. Is there a justification?   *Yes.*

IV. *Overall Evaluation of the Opinion*   *Reasonable.* Opinion reflects an awareness of the nature of the logic of democracy; majority rule, minority rights, political equality, and protection of political right by the Federal Courts.

Clark Opinion

Criteria

I. *Conceptual Framework*

    a. Nature of the Commit-   "Limited Pluralism"
       ment.

    b. Objective Sought   Providing relief when other chan-
                       nels are closed.

    c. Adequacy of the defini-   *Inadequate.* He defines the situa-
       tion of the situation   tion in a mathematical way only,
                       without raising the question:
                       blocking access to public policy.

II. *Technical Evaluation*

    a. Choices Perceived   1. Deny jurisdiction; 2. accept
                       and provide relief.

    b. Consequences Perceived   1. Crazy quilt pattern would con-
                       tinue; 2. rational scheme would
                       have to be developed.

    c. Adequacy of a. and b.   *Adequate.*

    d. Structure of the opinion   Logically consistent, plausible.

III. *Terms of the Justification*

    a. Good reasons offered?   *No.*

    b. Is there a justification?   *No.* While concurring with the
                       Brennan opinion, Clark's reasons
                       are inadequate.

IV. *Overall Evaluation of the*   *Unreasonable.* Opinion reflects a
    Opinion   view of democracy and represen-
                       tative government that does not
                       enable Clark to raise the empiri-
                       cal question of whether a major-
                       ity has been denied access to the
                       political process.

Frankfurter Opinion

Criteria

I. *Conceptual Framework*

a. Nature of the Commitment	"Judicial Restraint"/"Limited Pluralism"
b. Objective Sought	Protection of the Court's prestige and moral sanctions power.
c. Adequacy of the definition of the situation	*Inadequate.* Ignored the empirical question of who was blocking access to the political process.

II. *Technical Evaluation*

a. Choices Perceived	1. Deny jurisdiction; 2. accept jurisdiction and provide remedies.
b. Consequences Perceived	1. Court's prestige protected; citizen's redress of grievances lies elsewhere; 2. Court enters "political thicket" and its reputation tarnished.
c. Adequacy of a. and b.	*Inadequate.* Perceptions of consequences unrealistic.
d. Structure of the opinion	Rhetorical, plausible.

III. *Terms of the Justification*

a. Good reasons offered?	*No.*
b. Is there a justification?	*No.* Because the opinion flies in the face of societal commitments, political and legal, to principles of democracy and majority rule.

IV. *Overall Evaluation of the Opinion* — *Unreasonable.* Opinion does not raise the important question present in any discussion of democracy and representative government: Is an institutional arrangement to be allowed that blocks full and free debate on substantive public policy issues?

Harlan Opinion

Criteria

I. *Conceptual Framework*

    a. Nature of the Commitment.   "Judicial Restraint"/"Limited Pluralism"

    b. Objective Sought   Protection of the Court's prestige; maintenance of the Tennessee apportionment plan because it was reasonable.

    c. Adequacy of the definition of the situation   *Inadequate.* In that, while Harlan recognized the empirical conditions, he accepted the inequities as proper and rational.

II. *Technical Evaluation*

    a. Choices Perceived   Same as Frankfurter's choices.

    b. Consequences Perceived   1. The rational plan would continue; 2. Court's involvement would be a sorry day in that prestige of institution would drop.

    c. Adequacy of a. and b.   *Inadequate.* Ignored the obvious empirical consequences because he felt that legislatures ought to act in any manner they saw fit.

    d. Structure of the opinion   Consistent, plausible.

III. *Terms of the Justification*

    a. Good reasons offered?   *No.*

    b. Is there a justification?   *No.*

IV. *Overall Evaluation of the Opinion*   *Unreasonable.* Because, basically, his opinion is structured upon a commitment to democracy that denies fallibilism and open-endedness and stresses, instead, conservation of old ways and customs because they are there.

Stewart Opinion

> *No Judgment*. While Stewart expresses a latent "Limited Pluralism" his brief comments in *Baker*, reiterate the point that Brennan's opinion merely stated Court jurisdiction and justiciability and standing. Stewart sharply limited the intentions or the implications of the Brennan opinion (as he read the majority opinion).

*tion and strategy, standards were not set that officially pronounced the view.** The study now turns to the two cases that firmly established the Court's commitment to fallibilism, *Grey v. Sanders* and *Reynolds v. Sims*.

---

* Referring back to the previous note on page 122, one would be correct in stating that judicial caution and strategy accounted for the procrastination "technique" in *Baker*.

NOTES: CHAPTER 3

1. Royce Hanson, *The Political Thicket*, Englewood Cliffs, Prentice-Hall, 1966, pp. 41–42.
2. Glendon Schubert, *Judicial Policy-Making*, Chicago, Scott-Foresman and Co., 1965, p. 153.
3. Murphy, *op cit.*, p. 193; Schubert, *op cit.*, p. 150.
4. See Anthony Lewis, "Legislative Apportionment and the Federal Courts," LXXI *Harvard Law Review*, April 1958; Richard L. Strout, "The Next Election Is Already Rigged," Harper's Magazine, November, 1959.
5. *Dyer v. Kazuhisa Abe*, 138 *Fed. Supp.* 220 (1956).
6. *McGraw v. Donovan*, 159 *Fed Supp.* 901 (1958).
7. Hanson, *op cit.*, p. 42.
8. March 29, 1962, in Allan Lerman and Harold Chase, editors, *Kennedy and The Press*, New York, Thomas Crowell and Co., 1965, pp. 218–219.

9. "The Reapportionment Case," 76 *Harvard Law Review*, November 1962.
10. Schubert, *op cit.*, p. 152.
11. *Baker v. Carr*, 179 *Fed. Supp.* 824 (1959); *Scholle v. Hare*, 360 *Mich* 1,104 *N 2d* 63 (1960); *Asbury Park Press, Inc. v. Wooley*, 33 *NJ* 1, 161 *A2d* 705 (1960); *Maryland Committee for Fair Representation v. Tawes*, No. 13, 920 *Equity* (1961); *WMCA v. Simon*, 196 *Fed. Supp.* 758 (SD, NY, 1961).
12. *Baker v. Carr*, 369 *US* 186 (1961) at 187.
13. Hanson, *op cit.*, p. 53.
14. Brief for the US as Amicus Curiae on Reargument, *Baker v. Carr*, 369 *US* 186, pp. 21–78.
15. "Tennessee: Inertia in the Courts," in Jewell, ed., *op cit.*, pp. 314–325.
16. *Legislative Apportionment in Tennessee, 1901-1961*, Nashville, 1961.
17. *Baker v. Carr*, 369 *US* 186, at 194.
18. at 208.
19. at 208.
20. at 209.
21. at 210.
22. at 217.
23. at 215.
24. at 226.
25. at 226.
26. Jay A. Sigler, *An Introduction To The Legal System*, Homewood, Dorsey Press, 1968, pp. 26–27.
27. *Baker*, at 197.
28. at 198–204.
29. at 206.
30. at 198.
31. at 226.
32. at 217.
33. at 209.
34. at 244.
35. at 247, 249.
36. at 249.
37. at 244–245.
38. at 245.
39. at 249.
40. at 249.
41. at 248.
42. at 250.
43. *Asbury Park* (New Jersey), *McGraw* (Minn.).
44. Baker, at 245.

45. at 251.
46. at 258.
47. at 251–252.
48. at 252.
49. at 260.
50. at 261.
51. at 262.
52. at 262.
53. at 256.
54. at 252.
55. at 253.
56. at 254.
57. at 254.
58. at 255–56.
59. at 258.
60. at 259.
61. at 262.
62. at 260.
63. at 260.
64. at 265.
65. at 265.
66. at 266.
67. at 267.
68. at 267.
69. at 268.
70. at 278.
71. at 278.
72. at 280.
73. at 285.
74. at 300.
75. at 267.
76. at 268–269.
77. at 269.
78. at 323.
79. at 301.
80. at 299.
81. at 299–300.
82. at 300.
83. at 302–320; 321.
84. at 270.
85. at 289.
86. at 332, 334.
87. at 333.

88. at 346–347.
89. at 334.
90. at 334.
91. at 348.
92. at 348.
93. at 335.
94. 336
95. at 337.
96. at 337.
97. at 336.
98. at 331.
99. at 336.
100. at 340.
101. "Some Comments On the Reapportionment Cases," 63 *Michigan Law Review*, 243 (1964).
102. *Baker*, at 248 (fn 4).
103. at 253.
104. Felix Frankfurter, *Of Law and Men*, New York, Harcourt, Brace & Co., 1956, p. 58.
105. *Baker*, at 273.
106. at 273.
107. See p. 32.
108. Thorson, *The Logic of Democracy*, p. 160.
109. *Baker*, at 347, 348 (fn 9).
110. at 192.
111. at 193.
112. at 199.
113. See Murphy, *op cit.*, and Schubert, *op cit.*
114. *Baker*, at 201.
115. See Chapter 2, pp. 52–58.

4

Grey v. Sanders

INTRODUCTION

a. The Problems After Baker v. Carr

Professor McCloskey's prophecy, that the *Baker* decision
was a Pandora's box to be opened by a nationwide "latent
consensus," proved to be a correct one. After Baker came
a flood of petitions to state and federal courts regarding
state and congressional districting and apportionment
plans. Within a year, 75 cases had been filed in these
courts, many of them representing "an exuberant release
from the hopeless frustration which had been the hallmark
of past attempts at apportionment reform."[1] Within two
years of Baker, court cases demanding an end to malapportionment were filed or prosecuted in 41 states. In 26
states, Courts had found the apportionment of one or both
houses of the state legislatures involved in the litigation
to be unconstitutional. State courts upset existing appor-
tionments and ordered into effect or cleared the way for
new apportionment plans.

The essential problem after *Baker* thus arose: how to
produce a workable, judicially enforceable set of standards
of apportionment under the Equal Protection Clause of

the Fourteenth Amendment. Three other questions arose with regard to the basic one: these were concerned with (1) the latitude for legislative experimentation, that is, how much deviation from the equality of the Fourteenth Amendment was to be permitted, (2) whether the Equal Protection Clause required that both houses of a bicameral state legislature be apportioned on the basis of population, and (3) what if malapportionment is the consequence of a plan acceptable to a majority of the voters in an initiative or referendum election proposal.[2]

In *Grey v. Sanders,* a decision handed down in March of 1963, the Supreme Court majority opinion introduced the "one man, one vote" standard. It was shortly to become, a year later in the *Reynolds v. Sims* case, a fundamental constitutional requirement[3] applicable to all state legislative reapportionment plans. But first the background, opinions, and evaluation of the opinions in the Georgia case.

b. The Georgia Case, Grey v. Sanders

The issue in *Grey v. Sanders* (372 *US* 368) was simple enough: can a state employ a scheme of weighted voting in selecting representatives from one geographical constituency? The scheme used to weight the votes of some more heavily than others was the County Unit System, a system that had been part of Georgia politics since the days of the Civil War.

Each of Georgia's 159 counties was given (in the Georgia Constitution, Article III, Section III, Clause I), a certain number of votes: the eight largest counties, having three representatives, had twice the number (six) of unit votes; the thirty next largest counties, having two representatives, had four unit votes each, and the remainder, 121 counties, had one representative each, therefore two unit votes.[4]

The candidate who carried the county would win all its unit votes. The winner of these elections (Democratic primary elections in one-party Georgia) was the candidate with the largest number of county unit votes. However, given the way in which the Georgia districts had been drawn and representatives apportioned to these constituencies, a candidate could win the popular vote but lose the nomination by running poorly in rural areas which combined had more unit votes than the more populous areas.

At the time of the Court decision to hear the *Grey* case, the fifth appeal to the Supreme Court in fifteen years and the only successful one,[5] the rural areas of Georgia had completely dominated the politics of the state and rural political leaders had determined the makeup of the state legislatures as well as that of the Georgia congressional delegation for over fifty years. The county unit system may have had theoretical advantages "but failure to modify it to give added representation to emerging metropolitan areas led to the complete domination of state politics by the rural areas."[6]

In 1962, James O'Hear Sanders, a citizen and qualified voter in Fulton County (Atlanta), secured an injunction restraining Jim Grey, the Chairman of the Democratic State Executive Committee, from conducting elections under the County Unit System. The day the case came before the Federal District Court in 1962, the Georgia legislature modified the system as follows: Counties with populations not exceeding 15,000 received two unit votes (97 such counties), an additional unit for the next 5000 population (22 counties) ; an additional unit for the next 10,000; an additional unit for the next two brackets of 15,000, and thereafter, two more units for each increase of 30,000. Of the 159 Georgia counties, 119 of them did not exceed 20,000 in population and yet they held 260 unit votes (within 14 of a majority). The remaining 40 counties, ranging in population from 20,481 to 556,326 (Fulton County—Atlanta which had 6 unit votes of the total of 410—1.46% of the total although its population comprised 14.11% of Georgia's total), controlled 287 unit votes yet had a combined population totalling more than two-thirds of the state's total population. Even with the change, "combination of the units from the counties having the smallest population gives counties having population of one-third of the total in the state a clear majority of the county units."[7]

The District Court held that the system "as applied" violated the Equal Protection Clause of the Fourteenth Amendment and it issued an injunction "against conducting such an election under a county unit system that does not meet the requirements specified by the Court."[8] The specifications of the District Court did not call for one man, one vote. Instead, "it allowed a system to be used in weighting the votes if the system showed no greater disparity against a county than exists against any state in the conduct of national elections."[9] The State of Georgia then appealed the decision of the District Court. It moved to dismiss the injunction, alleging that the system was constitutional and was designed to "achieve a reasonable balance as between urban and rural electoral power."[10]*

---

* Subsequent to the District Court ruling, the Georgia Democratic Committee voted to hold the 1962 State primary for the statewide offices on a popular vote basis.

The Supreme Court, in accepting the case on appeal, moved closer to grappling with theories of political representation and to the critical task of establishing standards for apportionment of legislative seats. The opinions in *Grey* dealt with the question of weighted voting within a given constituency. This had to be resolved before coming to grips with the basic question of determining the nature of constitutionally valid election districts and apportionment processes. The opinions rendered in *Grey,* and the evaluation of them, now follow.

I. THE OPINIONS IN GREY V. SANDERS

a. The Douglas (Majority) Opinion

In the *Baker* case, Associate Justice William O. Douglas's concurring opinion maintained that "there is room for weighting" in state apportionment plans.[11] In the *Grey* case, now writing for a majority of the Court justices, Justice Douglas, for reasons to be discussed later, virtually ignored his earlier comments. The normative dimension of the Grey judgment is not at all complex. It is that "the conception of political equality from the Declaration of Independence, to Lincoln's Gettysburg Address, to the Fifteenth Amendment, the Seventeenth Amendment, the Nineteenth Amendment can mean only one thing—one person, one vote."[12]*

---

* Justice Clark acknowledged in the January 17, 1969 interview, that Douglas coined the phrase himself during the conference sessions. In a later interview with Justice William O. Douglas, he verified this fact—saying, in part, that he did not recall ever coming across that phrase in his reading of briefs, books on democracy, etc. Interview in his chambers, February 25, 1969.

While the states can specify the qualifications of voters in both state and federal elections,** they cannot deny blacks and women the right to vote, for that would be "non-allowable discrimination. How then can one person be given twice or ten times the voting power of another person in a statewide election merely because he lives in a rural area or because he lives in the smallest rural county?"[13] The Court, emphasized Douglas in this normative phase of the opinion, has consistently recognized "that all qualified voters have a constitutionally protected right to cast their ballots and have them counted at congressional elections. . . . Every voter's vote is entitled to be counted once,"[14] regardless of race, "whatever their sex, whatever their income, and wherever their home may be."[15]

At its core, the normative dimension's theme was that "once the geographical unit for which a representative is to be chosen is designated, all who participate in the election are to have an equal vote. . . . This is required by the Equal Protection Clause of the Fourteenth Amendment."[16] "The concept of 'We, the People' under the Constitution," maintained Douglas, "visualizes no preferred class of voters but equality among those who meet the basic qualifications."[17] There exists no provision in the Constitution that allows certain homesites or occupations greater voting power than other sites or professions. Therefore, "once the class of voters is chosen and their qualifications specified, we see no constitutional way by which equality of voting power may be evaded."[18]

** It should be noted, however, that on December 21, 1970, the Supreme Court, ruling on the constitutionality of the 1970 Voting Rights Act, legitimatized (1) the lowering of the voting age to 18 in Federal elections (*Oregon v. Mitchell*, 5-4) , (2) the establishment of a uniform 30-day residency requirement (*U.S. v. Arizona*, 8-1) , and (3) the removal of all literacy tests (*U.S. v. Idaho*, 9-0) .

With this normative view of the idea of political equality in mind, the technical and legislative dimensions of the *Grey* majority opinion fall into place. *Grey* was not, like *Baker*, a case involving the degree to which the Equal Protection Clause limits the authority of state legislatures in *designing geographical districts* from which representatives are then chosen. It did not involve racial gerrymandering to exclude minority groups from participating in municipal affairs (*Gomillion v. Lightfoot*, 364 *US* 339-1961), nor did *Grey* involve the question of whether one house of a bicameral legislature could be chosen without regard to population.[19] "Grey," said Douglas, "is only a voting case."[20]

Examining the evidence, the data presented earlier in this Chapter, Douglas noted that the state gave every voter one vote in the statewide elections. However, "in counting those votes she [Georgia] employs the county unit system which in end result weights the rural vote more heavily than the urban vote and weights some small rural counties heavier than other larger rural counties."[21]

Since the issue was a justiciable one in the Federal Courts, the alternative was either the retention of a system that violated the implicit command of "one person, one vote" in the Fourteenth Amendment's Equal Protection Clause, or judicial action in the absence of legislative action in order to ameliorate a flagrant constitutional violation of equal justice. Given the Constitution's categorical imperative (according to the normative conception held by Douglas of the meaning of "We The People"), the choice was clear. The opinion's legislative dimension, reflecting the normative commitment of the judges, vacated the judgment of the District Court, which allowed the county unit system so long as its weighted voting formula was less than or equal to the discrepancies that appeared in national weighted vote situations, e.g., Senatorial representation, electoral college, and remanded the case "so that a decree in conformity with our opinion may be entered."[22]

The justification for the decision was also a simple, basic justification for judicial action: "If it be a matter within our jurisdiction, we are bound by our oaths to judge of it."[23] Equality of voting was such a matter; therefore the Court felt obliged to hear the case and come to a judgment on the controversial issue.

b. The Stewart (Concurring) Opinion

Justice Stewart's concurring opinion was more a postscript addressed to the dissenting justice than an opinion. He reaffirmed the basic value judgment of the majority opinion. Rejecting the idea that *Grey* was somehow involved in questioning the validity of a State's apportionment scheme itself, Stewart argued (to Harlan) that the case "involves statewide elections of a United States Senator and of State executive and judicial officers responsible to a statewide constituency."[24] In this situation, Stewart said, "within a given constituency, there can be room for but a single constitutional rule—one voter, one vote."[25]

c. The Harlan (Dissenting) Opinion

To Justice Harlan, the Supreme Court majority's "one man, one vote" doctrine was "constitutionally untenable."[26] His normative assertions, echoing his and Justice Frankfurter's dissents in the *Baker* case, were (1) that the majority holding, that the Equal Protection Clause requires that each person's vote be given equal weight, "surely flies in the face of history,"[27] (2) that "state might rationally conclude that its general welfare was best served by apportioning more seats in the legislature to agricultural communities than to urban centers, lest the legitimate interests of the former be submerged in the the stronger electoral voice of the latter."

Furthermore, Harlan (3) "did not see how it can be deemed irrational for a state to conclude that a candidate for such office (State Executive) should not be one whose choice lies with the numerically superior electoral strength of urban voters," and (4) that it is therefore rational "to assure against a predominantly 'city point of view' in the administration of the State's affairs."[28]

Given Harlan's normative views, that is, that weighting is a rational policy and that the Equal Protection Clause, *in any case,* does not prohibit such rational action on the part of a state legislature, his technical and legislative conclusions that follow are not surprising.

Harlan maintained that, since the Equal Protection Clause is not violated "in the mere circumstance that the Georgia County Unit System results in disproportionate vote weighting,"[29] the system should be maintained as constitutional. Harlan realized (as he did in the *Baker* case) that, "at the core of Georgia's diffusion of voting strength, which favors the small as against the large counties, is the urban-rural problem so familiar in the American political scene."[30] His choice among the alternatives, voiding the scheme or retaining it, was a simple one— based on his normative commitments.

His legislative judgment, however, because Harlan was greatly concerned about the larger question of "a formulation of the basic ground rules in this untrod area of judicial competence,"[31] was more inconclusive than his technical evaluation. Harlan felt that the Court should address itself to the larger question of standards for judicial apportionment but that the *Grey* case was not a good vehicle for such a discussion because it was not a fully developed case.[32] "A more fully developed record" was necessary in order to demonstrate the constitutional untenability of the one man, one vote "ideology" of the majority. "A matter which so profoundly touches the barriers between federal judicial and state legislative authority demands nothing less."[33] Thus Harlan would have vacated the judgment of the District Court and would have remanded the case for a new trial: "The basic ground rules implementing *Baker v. Carr* should await the trial of this or some other case. . . . Only then can we know what we are doing."[34]*

II. THE EVALUATION OF THE OPINIONS

The opinions in *Grey* are quite revealing for two reasons, both related. For one thing, while the case did not directly touch upon the question of guidelines or standards for state districting and reapportionment but instead dwelt upon a problem that developed subsequent to districting and apportionment, it did establish a constitutional doctrine, the democratic belief in "one man, one vote."

Additionally, as Justice Harlan's dissent indicated, the

---

* It is important to note that Justice Harlan, both in the *Grey* opinion and in the interview with the author on February 25, 1969, insisted that *Grey* was part of the seamless web that began with *Baker* and that would end with "one man" firmly established as the constitutional standard in *all* districting and reapportionment cases.

conflict between the judicial activists and the lone dissenter took a new turn due to the fact that the Court
majority *seemed to indicate* the course of direction it
would follow when the apportionment issue rose again
before the Court.

As already indicated, strategy in controversial public
policy areas is one of procrastination, thus laying the
groundwork for future constitutional decisions.[35] Such
strategy is seen as reasonable because the justices correctly
perceived the situational context in which they functioned.

a. Conceptual Frameworks and Definitions of the Situation

The Douglas opinion's conceptual framework, responsible for (1) framing the definition of the situation, (2)
the technical and legislative aspects of the situation, and
(3) the justification for the Court's actions, stressed the
notion of majoritarianism. This ideal, found present in
the Black and Douglas dissents in *Colegrove* and in the
Brennan and Douglas opinions in *Baker,* was formalized
in the "one man, one vote" phrase coined by Douglas.
To the Justice, in *Grey,* the conception of *political equality* in voting meant only one thing—one man, one vote.
Equality in voting, according to Douglas, was a right that
is constitutionally protected, for once an area has been
designated there is "no constitutional way by which equality of voting power may be evaded."

This conceptual framework mirrors the normative
propositions in the model of democracy presented in
Chapter 1. By stressing political equality (in voting),
Douglas was opting for a judgment that stressed majority
rule and fallibilism. While it is true that Douglas did say,
in *Baker,* that there was room for weighting (as did Bren-

nan's opinion), no positive mention of weighting was present in this case. (Weighting per se would seem to be antithetical to the notion of political equality, and in upcoming cases the Court majority, although stating that mathematical equality is an impossibility, does not in any positive sense discuss weighting.)

As the matter was a justiciable issue, and the District Court's decision hedged on the constitutionality and the politics of the issue, Douglas and the Court majority felt that the Supreme Court should hear the case. The definition of the situation, in the Douglas opinion, was precise: *Grey* was a voting rights case. Douglas's opinion maintained, in the terms of the model of democracy, that the County Unit System of counting votes was a scheme that blocked access to the political process by those citizens in more heavily populated counties in the state of Georgia. Or, and this is important, that the plan could have blocked the *possibility* of representative government and the accompanying access to the political processes. And according to the model, neither the majority nor the minority of the population can block access to the political process, for to do so would be antidemocratic (assuming that we can use the terms "majority" and "minority").

How adequate is the definition of the situation? Insofar as there exist definite, identifiable "rural" and "urban" interests (and Justice Harlan in his dissent seems to feel this way), and homogeneous rural "minorities" and urban "majorities," then the Douglas definition is adequate. In Georgia, and other Southern and border states, one could say that there were, and still are, identifiable interests and masses—farming, city problems, minority, majority— and that Civil War and post-Civil War districting and apportionment formulas allowed the identifiable rural interests to control the legislative processes.[37] The Douglas opinion, then, without getting into the "Bugaboo of the majority" argument,[38] concluded that the County Unit System did block the access to the political process of the urban voters by diluting the value of their votes. (Georgia statistics are interesting with reference to this issue:[39] The largest Senatorial district in Georgia was 661.9% above the state average; the smallest 82.1% below the average. In the House, the corresponding figures were: 864% above, 90.2% below.)

The simple fact is that Georgia politics was controlled by the rural interests for over half a century, that Georgia delegations to the Senate reflected a particular constituency due to the weight given the rural voters and interests, that Georgia congressional delegations—based on district lines drawn by malapportioned legislatures—also reflected the rural orientation. This fact would indicate that the Douglas definition of the situation was adequate.

Justice Harlan's conceptual framework contradicted the majority opinion—as it did in the *Baker* decision. It was a normative assertion that contradicted the model of democracy presented earlier, for it asserted that the "one man, one vote" ideology was philosophically, constitutionally, and historically untenable, and that it was perfectly constitutional and rational for a state legislature to weight votes to "assure against a predominantly 'city point of view.' "

This conceptual framework confronts and conflicts with the notion that, in a democratic system, there shall be no intentional and institutional blocking of access by interested citizens to the political machinery—and this democratic admonition would include the blockage that exists as a result of intentional *mal*-apportionment.

The intent of the Georgia legislators was clear: to weight votes—dilute the strength of numbers in certain constituency sub-units of the state—to, using the words they spoke in their brief in the *Grey* case, "achieve a reasonable balance as between urban and rural electoral power."

Harlan's definition of the situation, given his limited pluralist stand conceptually, was such that he could state that weighting votes was in the general interest and for the general welfare of the state. Weighting is not unconstitutional; it is a natural consequence of the rural-urban problem, he claims in his opinion. But, as we shall see below, due to Harlan's conservative attitude on this public policy issue, he ignores the reality of weighted voting insofar as the theory of democracy is concerned.

Weighted voting does not aid the general welfare of the state if, due to the plan, legitimate interests, ideas, demands, and supports are not permitted to be raised because they are from the urban areas. His definition of the situation, then, is not adequate because the plan he defends as rational does not resolve the problem of conflict of interests (if this exists) ; *it ignores the problem!*

b. The Technical Evaluation and the Justification Phases

The Douglas opinion's technical evaluation of the situation, in terms of choices open to the Court for acting on the problem, was a simple one: either the Court, in its constitutional capacity as arbiter and resolver of disputes involving the principles of the Constitution and state statutes and constitutions, would intervene to rule that the County Unit System violated a cardinal individual civil right, or the Court would remain silent and by this silence condone the system of weighted voting (based on homesite) that represented a rejection of the fundamental principle of political equality.

In choosing the former alternative, involvement in the controversy, Douglas and the other judges of course did not maintain that the removal of the County Unit System would rid Georgia politics of all taint and allow representative opinions to be heard at all times.[40] The assumption behind the alternative chosen was more realistic, hence adequate in terms of the evaluation. It was that the Court, in attempting to narrow the gap between democratic Ideology and reality of democracy, acted to remove a particular obstacle—weighted voting. The judges, as active participants in the political process, knew that there were other obstacles—for example, the manner in which districts were created, seats apportioned, gerrymandering, noninvolvement of citizens even with political equality protected. But the judges acted reasonably in *Grey*, as they attempted to slowly, as they interpreted the Constitution, redirect the state's action in accordance with the Fourteenth Amendment.

"Evil there would be, corruption there would be, *even after* the 'one vote, one man' decision—but we must do a little to remove an identifiable injustice"—this could have been the reasoning of the justices in the majority.[41] As Justice Douglas mentioned in his earlier *Baker* opinion, hopefully these apportionment opinions of the Courts would have a "prophylactic effect" on state legislatures. (It would seem, moreover, that this technical evaluation has proven accurate. Emanuel Celler, commenting on these apportionment decisions, stated that the Court was "like a picador to the bull, and that the bull will never be the same again."[42])

The justification for the action of the Court in *Grey* was found in various documents from our history: the Declaration of Independence; the opening words of the Constitution—"We The People"; Lincoln's Gettysburg Address, the various amendments to the Constitution concerning voting equality (Fifteenth, Seventeenth, Nineteenth Amendments), and the nature of the judicial function itself in a democratic society. All the references to documents pointed to one democratic ideal: Government of, by, and for the people—regardless of race and sex. The function of the judiciary, the second basic reason for the action taken, is to act, according to the judges who participated in the formulation of the majority opinion, in those cases where its oath to ensure equal justice to all obliged the court—forced it—to act. Douglas was, in actuality,[43] saying that the duty of the Court was to act: "A right that a man has to give his vote at the election of a person to represent him in parliament, there to concur in the making of laws, which are to bind his liberty and property, is a most transcendent thing, and of an high nature. . . . It is a great injury to deprive him of it. . . . This right of voting is a right in the plaintiff by the common law, and consequently he shall maintain an action for the obstruction of it."[44]

Was the justification adequate because good reasons were presented? In the basic paradigm, good reasons were those that comported with standards of legal and political behavior. In the majority opinion, the reasons presented did parallel standards of behavior in these two areas: by acting the Court was (1) reinforcing basic American ideas regarding representative government (to argue, as the dissenting justices in the apportionment cases did, that because past American history did not act to reinforce these principles, the present Court should not begin to do so, is to refuse to face what Gunnar Myrdal wrote of as "The American Dilemma"[45]), and (2) acting in the highest legal manner possible, because it was following canons of judicial ethics, and acting to preserve basic legal-societal symbols.

Justice Harlan's technical evaluation and justification of his opinion is a different matter. As he indicated, in *Baker* and in *Grey*, the apportionment issue is a consequence of the urban-rural problem and that, in his judgment, it is perfectly rational for a state legislature to act in such a way as to limit the "representativeness" of certain areas by weighting (favorably) other, less populated areas. On the assumption that there are discernible differences of interests, the evaluation of the Harlan opinion rests upon the degree to which such state action ameliorates or heightens the rural-urban problem. (Certainly the County Unit System did not solve the problem—it disguised it; the County Unit System stalled action on the problem. But the problem of representativeness still remained—witness the number of Court appeals since 1945 by citizens living in urban areas.)

Judging by the consequences of malapportionment (as briefly mentioned in Chapter 2), it would seem that Georgia's case is no different from other Southern states that attempted to restrict urban residents and groups from fully participating in the political process.[46] That is, the Georgia County Unit plan for counting votes did not resolve the problem—it compounded the political problems. Justice Harlan's technical evaluation, that the plan was a rational consequence of the rural-urban dilemma and that the Court should therefore not rule it unconstitutional (the other alternative he saw), would seem to be inadequate.

It is inadequate because, as in the *Baker* opinion, his (1) commitment to the idea of limited pluralism, and his (2) narrow view of the judicial function forced him to base his judgment on these two normative assertions, assertions that did not allow or enable him to see the reality of the situation; that is, that repression does not solve a problem but merely delays it until it erupts in even greater strength than before.[47]

Furthermore, his technical evaluation, at the end, loses sight of the immediate problem, and instead raises an issue that (while related) was not immediately present: the basic question of standards of apportionment. Why Harlan would do this is not known at the moment. (However, as it was suggested earlier in this Chapter, Court strategy could have dictated that a case such as Grey could have come along—with the "one man, one vote" doctrine presented—before the Court had to tackle the basic question of standards for drawing up the districts and apportioning representatives to these units.) Whatever the reason for Harlan's discussion of standards, he used this point to come to the decision he reached: remanding the case in order to raise the larger question.

His justification would also seem to be inadequate. Justice Harlan does not present good reasons, nor even self-consistent reasons for his action. He ignores the ideals of American democracy which stress political equality— one man, every man, one vote—and he ignores, at the end, the issue raised in the case: voting rights and the possibility of their abridgment. At the core of his technical evaluation and justification, due to his normative commitments, was an ignorance of reality and the subsequent conflict between theory and reality. Justice Harlan was able to ignore such a reality because his conceptual framework emphasized minority representativeness to the detriment of majority rule. As has been maintained, the conceptual framework of the justices colors their image of the situation they face in judging. Because Harlan's framework did not stress open-endedness and did not adhere to to concept of "fallibilism," his opinion would seem to be both unreasonable and inadequate.

In these opinions, the judges of the Court continued their discussion of the meaning, nature, and dimensions of representative government and of political equality. In this continuing discussion, since *Colegrove,* two basic political philosophies had been expressed: the philosophy of majoritarianism and the philosophy of limited pluralism. In addition, the old discussion of the role of the judiciary was present from Colegrove on—that is, *should the Courts* and *to what extent* should the Courts get involved in this controversial issue of malapportionment. The first question had been answered in *Colegrove* and modified or clarified in *Baker.* The second question, at the time of *Grey,* was still an open one, although Justice Harlan seemed to feel that the Court was going to enter the fray all the way. The next Chapter deals with the second question. It also defines the meaning of "republican form of government." *Reynolds v. Sims,* decided in June of 1964, responded to the basic question of standards for apportionment. *Grey v. Sanders* provided the first clue regarding the direction the Court would take—a hint that was really born in the dissenting opinion of Justice Black in *Colegrove v. Green.*

FIGURE FIVE

Grey v. Sanders, 372 US 368

Criteria	Douglas Opinion	Harlan Opinion
I. Conceptual Framework		
a. Nature of the Commitment:	"Majoritarianism"	"Limited Pluralism"
b. "Objective Sought":	Protection of Voting Rights	Protection of the Court's Image; Weighted Voting
c. Adequacy of the Definition of the Situation	Adequate. Responded to the situation in a practical, realistic manner. Asked the question of who blocked access.	Inadequate. Responded to the situation by ignoring the fact that access was blocked by rural minority.
II. Technical Evaluation		
a. Choices Perceived:	Courts intervene to resolve constitutional conflict; violation of constitutional imperatives if Court remains silent.	Court intervenes with untenable "one man" concept; irrational system of weighted voting remains.
b. Consequences Perceived:	Continued violation of Constitution if no Court action.	Diminution of Court's power and respect if it intervenes in an essentially political problem.
c. Adequacy of a and b:	Adequate. Fallibilism indicated; data presented; fairness shown.	Inadequate. Harlan ignores the question of resolving the urban-rural problem; ignores past Court history regarding such questions.

d. Structure of the Opinion:	Well structured, consistent.	Inconsistent; poorly structured.
III. *Terms of the Justification*		
a. Is there a justification?	Yes. Good reasons offered. Standards of legal and political rationality presented.	No, because good reasons not presented.

NOTES: CHAPTER 4

1. Hanson, *op. cit.*, pp. 57–58.
2. *Ibid.*, pp. 60–63.
3. See Carl A. Auerbach, "The Reapportionment Cases: One Person, One Vote—One Vote, One Value," in Philip Kurland, editor, *The Supreme Court Review—1964*, Chicago: University of Chicago Press, 1964, pp. 1–88.
4. *Grey v. Sanders*, 373 US 368, at 370–371.
5. *Cook v. Fortson*, 1946; *Truman v. Duckworth*, 1946; *Cox v. Peter*, 1950; *Hartsfield v. Sloane*, 1958.
6. Albert B. Saye, "The Precedent Setter," 54 *National Municipal Review* 413, September 1965, 413–414.
7. From the District Court Opinion, in *Grey* at 373.
8. *Id.*
9. *Id.* at 374.
10. *Id.* at 370.
11. *Baker v. Carr*, 369 US 186, at 245.
12. *Grey v. Sanders*, 372 US 368, at 381.
13. *Id.* at 379.
14. *Id.* at 380.
15. *Id.* at 379.
16. *Id.*
17. *Id.* at 380.
18. *Id.* at 381.
19. *Id.* at 376.
20. *Id.* at 378.
21. *Id.* at 379.
22. *Id.* at 381.
23. *Id.* at 375, footnote 7 (quotation from Chief Justice Holt, 1702).
24. *Id.* at 382.
25. *Id.*
26. *Id.* at 390.
27. *Id.* at 384.
28. *Id.* at 386–387.
29. *Id.* at 386.
30. *Id.*
31. *Id.* at 389.
32. *Id.*
33. *Id.* at 390.
34. *Id.* See also Baker, *Reapportionment Revolution*, p. 125.
35. See, for example, the Supreme Court's handling of the miscegenation issue: *McLaughlin v. Florida* (1964); *Loving v. Virginia* (1967).

36. See W. Howard, Jr., "On the Fluidity of Judicial Choice," *op cit.*
37. Baker, *Reapportionment Revolution*, p. 50; Hugh D. Price, "Florida: Politics and the 'Pork Choppers,'" Preston Edsall, "North Carolina: People or Pine Trees," Malcolm Jewell, "Kentucky: A Latent Issue," all in Malcolm Jewell, editor, *The Politics of Reapportionment*, New York, Atherton Press, 1962, pp. 81–119; Howard Hamilton, et al, "Legislative Reapportionment In Indiana: Some Observations and a Suggestion," 35 *Notre Dame Lawyer*, 368–402, May 1960; Alvin Boskoff and Harmon Ziegler, *Voting Patterns in a Local Election*, New York, Lippincott Co., 1964, pp. 114–144; Terry Sanford, "The States and the Cities—The Unfinished Agenda," in Brian Berry and Jack Meltzer, editors, *Goals For Urban America*, Englewood Cliffs, Prentice-Hall, 1967, pp. 52–55; George Blair, *American Legislatures: Structure and Process*, Chapter 5, "Legislative Apportionment," pp. 77–108, New York, Harper and Row, 1967; J. Anthony Lukas, "Barnyard Government in Maryland," *op cit.*
38. Sidney Hook, *The Paradoxes of Freedom*, quoted in Auerbach, *op cit.*, p. 49.
39. See Chapter Two; The David and Eisenberg "Vote Value" Index, in Baker, *Reapportionment Revolution*, p. 59, indicates that the vote power of a citizen in DeKalb County, a suburban county in Georgia, went from 95 in 1910 to 23 in 1960 and that the value of the vote in Fulton County (the central city), Atlanta, Georgia, went from 24 in 1910 to 12 in 1960. 100 would indicate equitable vote value based on population of the county.
40. *In Metropolis Theatre Company v. Chicago*, 228 *US* 61, Justice Douglas wrote that "the problems of government are practical ones and may justify, if they do not require, rough accommodations—illogical it may be, and unscientific." At 69.
41. See, for example, Edmond Cahn, *The Nature of Injustice*, Bloomington, University of Indiana Press, 1959.
42. *Congressional Redistricting*, Hearings Before Subcommittee Number 5, Committee of the Judiciary, House of Representatives, Eighty Eighth Congress, Second Session, March 18–19, 1964, Washington, D.C., U.S. Government Printing Office, page 32.
43. See footnote 23.
44. *Ibid.*
45. Justice Felix Frankfurter and John W. Harlan, in particular.
46. See footnote 37 for references.
47. See Crane Brinton, *The Anatomy of Revolution*, New York, Vintage Books, 1965.

5

Reynolds v. Sims and
Post-Reynolds Judicial Actions

INTRODUCTION

a. From Grey to Reynolds

Grey v. Sanders, in which the "one man, one vote" concept was enunciated by the Court majority, was announced in March of 1963. Toward the end of 1963, the Supreme Court heard arguments surrounding two other issues in the apportionment controversy: On November 13, 1963, it listened to arguments regarding the apportionment of state legislatures (*Reynolds v. Sims*), and on November 18 and 19, 1963, it heard arguments with respect to the apportionment of congressional representatives (*Wesberry v. Sanders*). In February of the following year, the Supreme Court decision in the *Wesberry* case, also involving the state of Georgia, expanded the "one man, one vote" doctrine and made it a national standard insofar as congressional elections are concerned.

Writing for the Court majority, Justice Hugo Black maintained that the 1931 Georgia apportionment "grossly discriminates" against voters in the populous Fifth Con-

gressional District (Fulton County–Atlanta) : the apportionment statute "contracts the value of some votes and
expands that of others."[1] The opinion held that, "con-
strued in its historical context, the command of Article
I, Section 2, that Representatives be chosen 'by the people
of the Several States' means that as nearly as is practicable
one man's vote in a congressional election is to be worth
as much as another's. . . . To say that a vote is worth more
in one district than in another would not only run counter to our fundamental ideas of democratic government,
it would cast aside the principle of a House of Representatives elected 'by the People,' a principle tenaciously
fought for and established at the Constitutional Convention."[2] The opinion closed with the following standard:
"While it may not be possible to draw congressional
districts with mathematical precision, that is no excuse
for ignoring our Constitution's plain objective of making
equal representation for equal numbers of people the
fundamental goal for the House of Representatives. That
is the high standard of justice and common sense which
the founders set for us."[3]*

Justice Harlan, as in the earlier apportionment cases,
vigorously dissented, saying that he "had not expected to
witness the day when the Supreme Court of the United
States would render a decision which casts grave doubt
on the constitutionality of the composition of the House
of Representatives."[4] His basic complaint was this: "What
is done today saps the political process. The promise of
judicial intervention in matters of this sort cannot but

---

* To one observer, the Supreme Court "avoided prejudging the state reapportionment cases by basing its decision on Article I of the Constitution instead of the Fourteenth Amendment." Hanson, *op. cit.*, p. 72.
Justice Black told the author that he used Article I, rather than the
Fourteenth Amendment "because the former was less imprecise than
the latter."

encourage popular inertia in efforts for political reform through the political process, with the inevitable result that the process is itself weakened. By yielding to the demand for a judicial remedy in this instance, the Court in my view does a disservice both to itself and to the broader values of our system of government."[5]

Thus, while the Supreme Court was still formulating its decision on the question (the basic one) of state legislative districting, the *Wesberry* decision, handed down a few months before *Reynolds*, added another nail to the malapportionment coffin. The only question left, in this first round of discussion on apportionment that dealt with the major issues and general criteria, was this: what standards are constitutionally required when a state districts and apportions representatives for the state legislature?

Baker had established justiciability; *Grey* the "one man" principle regarding voters within a given geographical constituency; *Wesberry* extended "one man" so as to force, where necessary, state legislatures to redistrict and reapportion congressional districts and representatives on the basis of population equality. What was left for the Court to determine was the extent to which the "one man, one vote" doctrine would apply to state districting and apportionment.

The Supreme Court justices, at this time, were faced with a large number of reapportionment suits that came to state and federal courts following *Baker*—ushering in "a series of contradictory and irreconcilable decisions" as these various Courts, without standards established by the Supreme Court, went about implementing *Baker*.[6]

That the Court majority saw *Wesberry* as a part of a philosophical continuum is made clear in the *Reynolds* decision when Chief Justice Earl Warren stated that: [While *Grey* and *Wesberry*] "were based on different constitutional considerations, . . . neither are they wholly inapposite. *Grey* . . . established the basic principle of equality among voters in a state, and held that voters cannot be classified, constitutionally, on the basis of where they live, at least with respect to voting in statewide elections. And our decision in *Wesberry* . . . clearly established that the fundamental principle of representative government in this country is one of equal representation for equal numbers of people, without regard to race, sex, economic status, or place of residence within a state."[7]

Essentially, the *Reynolds* judicial discussions involved, as Justice Warren indicated, the question of whether or not there were any "constitutionally cognizable principles which would justify departures from the basic standard of equality among voters in the apportionment of seats in state legislatures."[8]*

b. The Alabama Case: The Basic Question Raised

Reynolds v. Sims, 377 *US* 533, 1964, was one of six cases heard by the Supreme Court regarding the issue of state legislative apportionment. The five other situations concerned apportionment problems in Virginia (*Davis v. Mann*), Delaware (*Roman v. Sincock*), Maryland (*Maryland Committee for Fair Representation v. Dawes*), New York (*WMCA v. Lomenzo*), and Colorado (*Lucas v. 44th General Assembly*). In August of 1961, a Mr. B. A.

---

* The opinion may also have reflected the judges' rejection of the "Holmes-Brandeis notion of States functioning as laboratories for social and economic experiments." Although the notion may have been "meritorious fifty years ago, [today it] no longer fits the most patent facts of political life."[9]

Reynolds and two other taxpayers and registered voters of Jefferson County, Alabama, brought suit in the Federal District Court for the Middle District of Alabama.

They sought to challenge the validity of the existing apportionment provisions of the state for electing state senators and members of the Alabama House of Representatives. They asked for a temporary injunction requiring the state to hold at-large elections in 1962.[10]

Reynolds's complaint alleged that, under the Alabama apportionment plan, citizens of the urban counties were being deprived of their rights under the Alabama Constitution and under the Equal Protection clause of the Constitution's Fourteenth Amendment. It further stated that the Alabama Legislature was composed of a Senate of 35 members and a House of 106 members. Under the 1961 Alabama Constitution, Article IX, Section 199, the Legislature was to reapportion the number of representatives among the citizens in accordance with the results of each decennial census of the United States, beginning in 1910.

The Constitution's next section (200), concerning state senators, stated that reapportionment should also take place after each decennial census, and the duty of the legislature was "to divide the state into as many senatorial districts as there are senators, which districts shall be as nearly equal to each other in the number of inhabitants as may be, and each shall be entitled to one senator, and no more."

Further, Article XVIII, Section 284, stated that "representation in the legislature shall be based upon population, and such basis of representation shall not be changed by constitutional amendments."

Reynolds had claimed, however, that the last apportionment plan of Alabama was based on the 1900 census figures, despite the requirements of the state constitution. "They asserted that, since the population growth in the state from 1900 to 1960 had been uneven, Jefferson and other counties were now victims of serious discrimination with respect to the allocation of legislative representation, (and that, in violation of both the state and the Federal Constitutions). They were denied 'equal suffrage in free and equal elections . . . and the equal protection of the laws.' "

There was no political way to right these wrongs, said the complaint, for the state's lawmakers would control the calling of and the activities of any proposed constitutional convention, and the state judiciary refused to intervene "with matters of legislative reapportionment." (Under the Alabama plan in existence in 1961, state senate districts varied in population from 15,417 to 634,-864 and the population per representative in the State House ranged from 6731 to 634,864.)

The three-judge District Court heard testimony from both sides, viewed the 1901 Apportionment plan and the two substitutes hastily drawn by the Alabama state legislators—the Crawford–Webb Act and an Amendment which would have created a 67 man senate—and declared that "each of the legislative acts, when considered as a whole, is so obviously discriminatory, arbitrary and irrational that it becomes unnecessary to pursue a detailed development of each of the relevant factors of the (Federal) constitutional test." The District Court pointed out that, under the new plans, and using the 1960 census figures, only 25.1 percent of the state's total population resided in districts represented by a hypothetical majority of the members of the Senate (25.7 percent was the corresponding figure for the House majority) .

The District Court found the so-called "Federal Analogy" used by the state legislators irrelevant. But the three man Court did not find, could not find, an adequate remedy for the problem of malapportionment. Instead the Court enjoined any future elections under any of the apportionment plans held to be invalid and it ordered a temporary reapportionment plan used for the 1962 elections.

It stated that it was retaining jurisdiction and deferring action on the request of Reynolds for a permanent injunction. Its moderate action, the District Court said, was "designed to break the strangle hold by the smaller counties on the Alabama legislature and would not suffice as a permanent apportionment." Its ruling was that 1962 would be the last election year in which elections would be held under a discriminatory reapportionment plan. The election was held, but the new legislators did not enact a reapportionment plan in accordance with the District Court's wishes.

Since "no effective political remedy to obtain relief against the alleged malapportionment appeared to have been available (there is no initiative procedure available, there is a difficult constitutional amending process, and a constitutional convention can be convened only after a convention call was issued after approval by both houses of the Alabama legislature) ," the Supreme Court felt that the Reynolds appeal was "timely filed," and the crucial and fundamental issue of reapportionment—the central question of criteria for reapportioning state legislatures in the light of the Equal Protection clause—finally came before the Supreme Court judges.

I. THE OPINIONS IN REYNOLDS V. SIMS

a. *The Warren (Majority) Opinion*

Chief Justice Earl Warren wrote the majority opinion of the Court in this watershed case; a case described by *The New York Times* as a radical decision of "historic importance. Not since the school segregation cases ten years ago had the Court interpreted the Constitution to require so fundamental a change in this country's institutions." Indeed, the *Times* concluded that *Reynolds* was one of the Supreme Court's "most far-reaching decisions since *Marbury v. Madison* established its power of judicial review in 1803."[11] The normative dimension of the opinion, as already indicated, continued on the majoritarian path developed by Justices Black, Brennan, and Douglas since Black's dissent in *Colegrove*.

"Undeniably the Constitution of the United States protects the right of all qualified citizens to vote, in state as well as in federal elections," began Warren.[12] American history traces the pattern of broadened suffrage rights, "and the right of suffrage can be denied by a debasement or dilution of the weight of a citizen's vote just as effectively as by wholly prohibiting the free exercise of the franchise."[13] The normative dimension of the majority opinion had these other substantive commitments:

(1) "Undoubtedly, the right of suffrage is a funda-

mental matter in a free and democratic society. Especially since the right to exercise the franchise in a free and unimpaired manner is preservative of other basic civil and political rights, any alleged infringement of the right of citizens to vote must be meticulously and carefully weighed."[14]

(2) "Representative government is in essence self-government through the medium of elected representatives of the people, and each and every citizen has an inalienable right to full and effective participation in the political processes of his state's legislative bodies. . . . Full and effective participation by all citizens [means that] each citizen have an equally effective voice in the election of members of his state legislature. Modern and viable state government needs, and the Constitution demands, no less."[15]*

(3) "Logically, in a society ostensibly grounded on representative government, it would seem reasonable that a majority of the people of a State could elect a majority of that State's legislators. To conclude differently, and to sanction minority control of state legislative bodies, would appear to deny majority rights in a way that far surpasses any possible denial of minority rights that might otherwise be thought to result."[16]

(4) Legislatures should be bodies which are collectively responsible to the popular will. "And the concept of equal protection has been traditionally viewed as requiring the uniform treatment of persons standing in the same relation to the governmental action questioned or challenged."[17]

(5) "Legislators represent people, not trees or acres. Legislators are elected by voters, not farms or cities or economic interests. As long as ours is a representative form of government, and our legislatures are those instruments of government elected directly by and directly

---

* This view parallels the concern of Walter Lippmann, who wrote that "without the intervention of the Court to push the states off dead center, the American political system may become paralyzed." In Baker, *Reapportionment Revolution*, pp. 138–139.

representative of the people, the right to elect legislators in a free and unimpaired fashion is a bedrock of our political system."[18]

(6) "One must be ever aware that the constitution forbids 'sophisticated as well as simple-minded modes of discrimination.' "[19]

(7) "To the extent that a citizen's right to vote is debased, he is that much less a citizen. The fact that an individual lives here or there is not a legitimate reason for overweighting or diluting the efficacy of his vote."[20]

(8) Though the character of a nation changes, the "basic principle of representative government remains, and must remain, unchanged—the weight of a citizen's vote cannot be made to depend on where he lives."[21]

(9) "Population is, of necessity, the starting point for consideration and the controlling criterion for judgment in legislative apportionment controversies. A citizen, a qualified voter, is no more nor no less so because he lives in the city or on the farm. This is the clear and strong command of our Constitution's Equal Protection Clause. This is an essential part of a government of laws and not men. This is at the heart of Lincoln's vision of 'government of the people, by the people, [and] for the people.' The Equal Protection clause demands no less than substantially equal state legislative representation for all citizens, of all places as well as of all races."[22]

(10) "While mathematical nicety is not a constitutional requisite, one could hardly conclude that the Alabama house, under the proposed constitutional amendment, had been apportioned sufficiently on a population basis to be sustainable under the Equal Protection Clause."[23]

(11) "Since the achieving of fair and effective representation for all citizens is concededly the basic aim of legislative apportionment, we conclude that the Equal Protection Clause guarantees the opportunity for equal

participation by all voters in the election of state legislators. Diluting the weight of votes because of place of residence impairs basic constitutional rights under the Fourteenth Amendment just as much as invidious discriminations based on factors such as race."[24]

(12) "The Equal Protection Clause requires that a state make an honest and good faith effort to construct districts, in both houses of its legislatures, as nearly of equal population as is practicable."[25]

(13) "We realize that it is a practical impossibility to arrange legislative districts so that each one has an identical number of residents, or citizens, or voters. Mathematical exactness is hardly a workable constitutional requirement."[26]

(14) "We hold that, as a basic constitutional standard, the Equal Protection Clause requires that the seats in both houses of a bicameral state legislature must be apportioned on a population basis. Simply stated, an individual's right to vote for state legislators is unconstitutionally impaired when its weight is in a substantial fashion diluted when compared with votes of citizens living in other parts of the State."[27]*

The Chief Justice's normative conception, elaborating on the nature of representative government, the right to vote (and its meaning), the nature of "representativeness" in a democracy, the meaning and (new) dimension of the Equal Protection Clause, and the responsibilities of the State legislators to their constituents and to the Federal Constitution, left no doubt as to the fact that a majority of the Court believed that the "one man, one vote" doctrine was to be the normative standard with regard to criteria for reapportioning legislative assemblies on the state and federal level.

---

* At another point in the opinion, Warren said that "our constitutional system amply provides for the protection of minorities by means other than giving them majority control of state legislatures" (at 566).

Using the "one man" doctrine as the normative value, the majority opinion's definition of the situation found that, while "state legislatures, are, historically, the fountainhead of representative government in this country,"[28] "legislative apportionment in Alabama is signally illustrative and symptomatic of the seriousness of (the problem of malapportionment) in a number of the states."[29] Presenting statistics, Warren indicated that the existing apportionment plan in Alabama "presented little more than crazy quilts, completely lacking in rationality and could be found invalid on that basis alone."[30]

The problem of malapportionment is a basic problem for a democratic society undergoing shifts from a basically rural to an urban and then to an urban-suburban society, noted the Chief Justice. It is evident by the growing number of cases coming before the Courts since the 1962 *Baker* decision.[31] And the problem the Supreme Court had to face, it seemed to Warren, was to determine the basic standards and to set the basic guidelines for implementing the *Baker* decision.

In Alabama's case, the Chief Justice said, it was easy to spot the unconstitutionality of the apportionment plans. The discrimination was easily spotted mathematically: "Two, five, or 10 of them [urban voters] must vote before the effect of their voting is equivalent to that of their favored neighbor."[32] Given the normative framework and the examination of the statistics in the Alabama case, Warren concluded that[33]

it would appear extraordinary to suggest that a State could constitutionally be permitted to enact a law providing that certain of the State's voters could vote two, five, or 10 times for their legislative representatives, while voters voting elsewhere could vote only once. And it is inconceivable that a state law to the effect that, in counting votes for legislators, the votes of citizens in one part of the state would be multiplied by two, five, or 10, while the votes of persons in another area would be counted at only face value, could be constitutionally sustainable. Of course, the effect of state legislative districting schemes which give the same number of representatives to unequal numbers of constituents is identical.

Warren observed that "our constitutional system amply provides for the protection of minorities by means other than giving them majority control of state legislatures";[34] that the State's defense—it was emulating the formula worked out in 1787 regarding area representation in the Senate and population representation in the House, that is, the Federal Analogy—is "inapposite and irrelevant to state legislative districting schemes";[35] that the constitutional standard announced in the case did not render the concept of bicameralism "anachronistic and meaningless," for "the prime reason for bicameralism, modernly considered, is to insure mature and deliberate consideration of, and to prevent precipitate action on, proposed legislative measures."[36]

Furthermore, the Warren opinion stated that "while dicennial reapportionment is not a constitutional requisite, compliance with such approach would clearly meet the minimal requirements for maintaining a reasonably current scheme of legislative representation";[37] and that "it may be feasible to use political subdivision lines to a greater extent in establishing state legislative districts than in congressional districting while still affording adequate representation to all parts of the state. To do so would be constitutionally valid, so long as the resulting apportionment was one based substantially on population and the equal-protection principle was not diluted in any significant way."[38]

In *Reynolds,* the definition of the situation, that is, state legislative reapportionment standards, was extensively explored by the Chief Justice. Finding malapportionment present in Alabama and other states, the situation thus defined placed the blame, and the responsibility for rectifying the situation, on the state legislatures.

As for the choice among alternatives the Court majority had to make in the Reynolds case, the technical evaluation aspect of the Warren opinion referred to the impairment of the petitioner's constitutionally protected rights demands judicial protection; our oath and our office require no less of us."[39]

The Equal Protection Clause requires that a state apportion its legislature on the basis of population; it is a constitutionally protected right and, therefore, the Court had no choice but to hear the case and decide according to the "neutral principle" in the Constitution. The alternative choice was anathema for the Court majority, that is, ignoring the violation of the Constitution by the Alabama state legislators: "The right of a citizen to equal representation and to have his vote weighted equally with those of all other citizens in the election of members of one house would amount to little if States could effectively submerge the equal-population principle in the apportionment of seats in the other house."[40]

The choice was seen as a clear-cut one: either carry out the judicial oath or ignore it. The consequences of the choices were also perceived with clarity: judicial action would force states that are malapportioned to reapportion in accordance with the one vote, one man doctrine whereas judicial inaction would lead to deadlock, paralysis and decay in state legislatures.

The Warren opinion therefore concluded that the District Court acted properly, that "the action taken . . . was an appropriate and well-considered exercise of the judicial power" (that is, the retention of jurisdiction while deferring a hearing on the issuance of a final injunction in order to give the provisionally reapportioned legislature an opportunity to act effectively) , and, since the District Court "avowedly intends to take some further action" should the Alabama legislature not reapportion for the 1966 elections, therefore the lower Court's actions were affirmed and the case remanded for further action consistent with the views expressed by the majority.[41]

The justification for the Court's action, according to Warren, lay in the nature of the judicial function in a representative democracy. "Only when validly asserted constitutional rights could not otherwise be protected and effectuated" should courts "attempt to accommodate the relief ordered to the apportionment provisions of state constitutions insofar as is possible."[42] Also, "when there is an unavoidable conflict between the Federal and a State Constitution, the Supremacy Clause of course controls,"[43] wrote Warren—with the evident implication that it is the Federal judiciary that determines the presence of the conflict in the first place. Simply put, the justification for the action was the oath the Supreme Court justices took to support the Constitution and the judicial oath to do justice at all times.[44]

b. The Clark (Concurring) Opinion

In a brief concurring opinion, Mr. Justice Tom Clark

took issue with the Warren conceptual framework, that is, the ideal of "majoritarianism." Clark felt that the Court majority was wrong in developing the "one man" doctrine into a basic constitutional standard for state legislatures when they reapportion.* Referring to his opinion in *Baker,* he maintained that all the Court had to do in the present case was to say "that each plan considered by the trial court is 'a crazy quilt,' clearly revealing invidious discrimination in each house of the legislature and therefore violative of the Equal Protection Clause."[45]

Contrary to the majority opinion, Clark was of the opinion that: "if one house of a state legislature meets the population standard, representation in the other house might include some departure from it so as to take into account, on a rational basis, other factors in order to afford some representation to the various elements of the state."[46] Simply put, the Court "goes much beyond the necessities of this case in laying down a new 'equal population' principle for state legislative apportionment."[47] However, because there is, in Clark's eyes and based on his normative conception as stated in *Baker,* a crazy quilt pattern and invidious discrimination, the District Court took the correct action in removing the apportionment plans.

c. The Stewart (Concurring) Opinion

Justice Potter Stewart's opinion agreed with the final result of the Warren opinion. Stewart, however, reached

---

* In his extended interview with the author, Justice Clark repeatedly expressed fear about "the tyranny of the urbanites" replacing the "tyranny of the ruralites." The justice consistently referred to the urban-rural dichotomy without ever discussing the political heterogeneity of "urban" environments, nor discussing the relationships between suburban and urban legislators.

the same conclusion, that is, that there was a violation of the Equal Protection Clause, by taking a different road. Stewart stated that the Fourteenth Amendment's equal protection clause demanded two things or attributes "of any plan of state legislative apportionment. First, it demands that, in the light of the state's own characteristics and needs, the plan must be a rational one. Secondly, it demands that the plan must be such as not to permit the systematic frustration of the will of a majority of the electorate of the State."[48] Therefore, if a reapportionment plan "could be shown to reflect no policy, but simply arbitrary and capricious action or inaction, and that any plan which could be shown systematically to prevent ultimate effective majority rule, [it] would be invalid under accepted Equal Protection Clause standards."[49]

What Stewart strenuously objected to was the Court majority's action converting "a particular political philosophy into a constitutional rule, binding upon each of the fifty states, from Maine to Hawaii, without regard and without respect for the many individualized and differentiated characteristics of each State, characteristics stemming from each State's distinct history, distinct geography, distinct distribution of population, and distinct political heritage. . . . [It is] the fabrication of a constitutional mandate which imports and forever freezes one theory of political thought into our Constitution, and forever denies to every State any opportunity for enlightened and progressive innovation in the design of its democratic institutions, so as to accommodate within a system of representative government the interests and aspirations of diverse groups of people, without subjecting any group or class to absolute domination by a geographically concentrated or highly organized majority."[50]

d. The Harlan (Dissenting) Opinion

Justice Harlan vigorously dissented in this and the other five cases handed down by the Court majority on June 15, 1964.* *Reynolds*, he said, "has the effect of placing basic aspects of state political systems under the pervasive overlordship of the federal judiciary [and once again], I must register my protest." He believed that the holding of the majority—"whatever may be thought of it as a piece of political ideology"—was not a political tenet imposed by the Fourteenth Amendment on the states, nor did the Amendment "authorize this Court to do so."

If the majority had "paused more deeply into the matter, they would have found that the Equal Protection Clause was never intended to inhibit the States in choosing any democratic method they pleased for the apportionment of their legislatures."[51] "This is shown," Harlan wrote, "by the language of the Amendment taken as a whole, by the understanding of those who proposed and ratified it, and by the political practices of the States at the time the Amendment was ratified."[52]

Harlan presented a lengthy history of the language, proposal, and ratification, history after 1868 to the present of the Fourteenth Amendment, proving that the majority opinion was amending the meaning of the Fourteenth Amendment, and that Congress did not restrict the State's power to control voting rights.[53] Harlan did maintain that State apportionment plans were wholly free of constitutional limitations, "save such as may be imposed by the Republican form of government Clause (Article IV)."

---

* The other apportionment opinions announced on June 15, 1964 were: *WMCA v. Lomenzo* 377 *US* 633 (1964); *Maryland Committee v. Tawes* 377 *US* 656 (1964); *Davis v. Mann* 377 *US* 678 (1964); *Roman v. Sincock* 377 *US* 695 (1964); *Lucas v. Colorado* 377 *US* 713 (1964).

The consequence of the Court's new "constitutional doctrine," a doctrine which indicated how far the majority had strayed "from the appropriate bounds of its authority," was that state courts "are given blanket authority and the constitutional duty to supervise apportionment of the State legislatures. It is difficult to imagine a more intolerable and inappropriate interference by the judiciary with the independent legislatures of the States." The decisions, he continued, "present a jarring picture of Courts threatening to take action in an area which they have no business entering, inevitably on the basis of political judgments which they are incompetent to make."[54]

Continuing his critique of the majority opinion, and indicating his own conceptual framework that stressed the twin concepts of federalism and judicial restraint, Harlan stated that "generalities cannot obscure the cold truth that cases of this type are not amenable to the development of judicial standards. No set of standards can guide a Court which has to decide how many legislative districts a state shall have, or what the shape of the districts shall be, or where to draw a particular district line."[55]

More explicit now, Harlan's normative commitments previously expressed in *Baker, Grey,* and *Wesberry,* came out when he pointed out ten factors which the Warren opinion excluded from consideration by a state legislature when it had to reapportion. The ten were history; economic or other group interests; area; geographical considerations; a desire to ensure effective representation for sparsely settled areas; availability of access of citizens to their representatives; theories of bicameralism; occupation; attempts to balance urban and rural power; preference of the majority of the voters in a state (referring to the Lucas decision). Harlan "knew of no principle of logic or practical or theoretical politics, still less any constitutional principle, which establishes all or any of these exclusions. The Court majority had reduced people to ciphers, but it was meaningful to note that people are not ciphers and that legislators can represent their electors only by speaking for their interests—economic, social, political—many of which do reflect the place where the electors live."[56]

His definition of the situation was a simple one: there was no state violation of the Equal Protection Clause. His technical evaluation was a pessimistic one: "What is done today deepens my conviction that judicial entry into this realm is profoundly ill-advised and constitutionally impermissible. . . . I believe that the vitality of our political system, on which in the last analysis all else depends, is weakened by reliance on the judiciary for political reform; in time a complacent body politic may result."[57] Harlan maintained that the erosion of the "fabric of federalism" was present in these apportionment decisions of the Court. Furthermore:[58]

these decisions give support to a current mistaken view of the Constitution and the constitutional function of this Court. This view, in a nutshell, is that every major social ill in this county can find its cure in some constitutional "principle," and that this court should "take the lead" in promoting reform when other branches of government fail to act. The Constitution is not a *panacea* for every blot upon the public welfare, nor should this Court, ordained as a judicial body, be thought of as a general haven for reform movements. The Constitution is an instrument of government, [and a fundamental premise] is that in a diffusion of governmental authority lies the greatest promise that this nation will realize liberty for all its citizens. [And] when, in the name of constitutional interpretation, the Court adds something to the Constitution that was deliberately excluded from it, the Court in reality substitutes its view of what should be so for the amending process.

In sum, Harlan's dissent, based on his view of "limited pluralism," federalism, judicial restraint, as well as his overriding belief in the ideal of federalism, (1) reaffirmed his earlier pronouncements on the apportionment issue, as it (2) condemned the Court for "amending" the Constitution and (3) debunked the "one man, one vote" ideology that was established by the Court majority as being constitutionally untenable. His perception of the situation, and his technical evaluation, followed his initial commitment to the normative assertions mentioned above. Harlan would have dismissed the complaints of Reynolds and would have reversed the decision of the District Court.

II. THE EVALUATION OF THE OPINIONS

The *Reynolds* opinion did establish a general constitutional standard with respect to state legislative reapportionment: districts were to be created and legislative seats were to be apportioned to these districts using population as the fundamental and controlling factor—for both houses of a bicameral state legislature. The Supreme Court majorities, in *Baker, Grey, Wesberry,* and *Reynolds,* agreed that the apportionment issue was justiciable and that, in order to give meaning to the idea of democratic government (and to give new life to the idea of Federalism by forcing a reexamination of the nature, role, and structure of state legislatures and state legislative processes), the "one man, one vote" standard was raised so as to be incorporated into the Equal Protection Clause of the Fourteenth Amendment.

The constitutional standard the Court created, however, was not as dogmatic as critics make it out to be.[59] "By inference at the very least, the Court decided to judge [future apportionment] cases individually rather than lay down a single, unambiguous and inflexible standard which all states must meet."[60] As already seen, there are rules of thumb for judicial use outlined in *Reynolds:* in particular (1) that the states make an "honest and *good faith* effort" to apportion fairly; (2) that the states be granted flexibility with respect to the use of local jurisdictional lines (historic boundaries), (3) that the principle of "mathematical exactness" is not a constitutional command, and (4) that there be no restriction on the type of district created (multi-member, single member, floterial).

As will be noted in the evaluation of the opinions and in Part III of this Chapter, *Reynolds* did not close the book on apportionment questions. Complex questions still existed after the June 1964 decisions. For example, if "population" is the standard, does population mean registered voters, or citizens, or total population of a state? If deviation is allowable, how much deviation? What about the issue of substate apportionment? Should school boards be based on the "one man, one vote" principle?[61] What about governmental units such as counties, towns, city councils? What about the question of gerrymandering? The issue of remedies? In short, the Court decisions, while establishing a constitutional guideline where none had existed (specifically) before, were not expected by the judges to answer, once and for all time, all questions surrounding reapportionment.

The Warren opinion did not spell out, because it "deemed it expedient not to," "any precise constitutional tests": "lower courts can and assuredly will work out more concrete and specific standards for evaluating state legislative apportionment schemes in the context of actual litigation. . . . What is marginally permissible in one State may be unsatisfactory in another, depending upon the particular circumstances of the case. Developing a body of doctrine on a case-by-case basis appears to us to provide the most satisfactory means of arriving at detailed constitutional requirements in the area of state legislative apportionment."[62]

The basic theme was sounded, however, by the Court majority: "one man, one vote—one vote, one value" was a necessary and vital institutional value in a society that based its political activities on the principles of universal suffrage and the representative assembly.[63]

a. Conceptual Frameworks and Definitions of the Situation

The Warren opinion's conceptual framework thoroughly accepts the premise of "majoritarianism" as the basis for representative government in a democracy, even to the extent of ruling unconstitutional a majority's action, in Colorado, that established a "little Federal Plan" rather than an apportionment plan based on population alone. (Warren had written that "the fact that an apportionment plan is adopted in a popular referendum is insufficient to sustain its constitutionality. The individual's constitutionally protected right to cast an equally weighted vote cannot be denied even by a vote of a majority of a state's electorate."[64]

Voting rights, according to the majority opinion, are

fundamental in a society that calls itself free and democratic, for they are the key to other basic civil and political rights. This view parallels the concept of "fallibilism" and "open-endedness" discussed in the first chapter. The right to vote, and to have effective representation based on population, does not mean that all major problems will be resolved. It does mean that, in approaching the problems of a society, the people in a state are adequately and equitably represented by legislators on the basis of population equality.

Blocking access to the legislative processes of government, according to the Warren conceptual framework, is *per se* undemocratic and elitist in nature. And a malapportioned state legislature did block access by diluting the value of the urban and suburban citizens vote, stated the Chief Justice. If equal representation for equal numbers of people is the basic principle of representative government in America, then this principle must remain unchanged so that the political process could function in a legitimate, constitutional fashion. Warren maintained that the decay of state legislatures was due to the rural stranglehold on the legislative machinery and that the "one man" standard would breathe fresh air and life into the politics of the states. Warren did not concern himself with output, that is, that well-apportioned legislatures would be more generous with social welfare programs; his opinion stressed only the means, the necessity for the existence of the democratic institutional value of "majoritarianism." As such, to reiterate, his opinion mirrored the idea of "fallibilism" and "open-endedness."

The Warren opinion's definition of the situation was an extremely perceptive, empirically-oriented one. The Court's awareness of political reality and the limits of judicial action are quite apparent when reading the Warren opinion. It was an opinion that showed an awareness of the rapid changes taking place in American society, of the shift from a rural to an urban to a metropolitan society, an awareness of the important role of the state legislatures in the federal system (and of the need to force the state legislatures to change their representational base so as to enter the new world of the mid-twentieth century).

Warren's opinion indicated the judiciary's alertness to the necessity of having state legislatures apportion themselves—rather than having the courts apportion them (but also aware that legislators would be quite reluctant to reapportion themselves out of power)—as well as indicating an awareness of the differences that exist in the various states that made the development of precise constitutional tests to determine malapportionment "inexpedient" (an awareness that the dissenting justices overlooked in their condemnation of the Warren opinion). It was, finally, an opinion that left the question of remedies available in case of malapportionment flexible rather than rigid, because of the general awareness that state strength in a Federal system must be maintained. For all these factors the opinion should be judged adequate.

Distinguishing between party structure and functions and pressure group structure and functions, the Warren opinion adequately determined that minorities have other means of protecting their interests than securing control of state legislatures. The point raised by Warren—pressure group activity within the political system, for example, lobbying before legislative committees, Courts, and bureaucratic agencies—is a political factor totally ignored by the dissenting justices.

Specifically, the Warren definition of the Alabama situation, based on the concept of "one man, one vote," clearly indicated that the standard was not being adhered to by the state legislators. (It is interesting to note that Warren stated that he could have used the "crazy quilt" criterion of Clark—and Stewart—and that this criterion would have been enough to strike down the Alabama apportionment plan. Instead, he chose to use, because of his commitment to "majoritarianism," the constitutional doctrine that had been first introduced in *Grey*.) * The state had not apportioned in over sixty years, and the apportionment plans turned down by the District Court favored the rural areas of the state, especially those in the "black belt."[65] Voting rights were being debased by the continual refusal of the Alabama legislature to reapportion—as its own state constitution required the legislators to do every ten years. (And, even after the *Reynolds* decision, only by the threat in July of 1965 that the District Court would reapportion the state legislature were the Alabama legislators forced to meet in special session in September of 1965 to pass a plan reapportioning the Senate and the House. The Alabama legislature had failed to reapportion in earlier regular and special sessions.)

Justice Clark's conceptual framework, implicitly expressed in his brief concurring opinion in *Reynolds* and in his agreement with Justice Stewart's dissenting opinion in *Lucas*, was a repetition of his normative assertions in *Baker v. Carr*. Clark maintained that the Equal Protection Clause disallowed only state legislative apportionment

---

* In the interview with the author, Justice Clark attested to this view of the Chief Justice regarding the usefulness of the "crazy quilt" device as a standard for determining the constitutionality of an apportionment statute.

schemes that were arbitrary, "crazy quilt" type patterns showing no rationality. He argued, in *Baker* and in *Reynolds,* that there could be a departure from the population standard in favor of interest or group representation and that this was a perfectly rational state policy not restricted by the Constitution. In short, his conceptual framework rejected the primacy of "majoritarianism" as a basic constitutional standard and opted instead for any *rational* state reapportionment scheme so long as it was not arbitrary and capricious.

In the *Reynolds* case, Clark's definition of the situation, based on his "crazy quilt" definition, was similar to the majority opinion but was arrived at using a different orientation. In the light of the conception of democracy discussed in the initial chapter, and for the same reasons raised earlier in the *Baker* evaluation, the Clark opinion, on the basis of the prior discussions of democracy and political equality, would be adjudged inadequate due to his conceptual framework.

The Stewart opinion, due to the criteria discussed in the first chapter, meets and merits the same evaluational judgment. It, too, is inadequate (even though, in *Reynolds,* it came to the same conclusion) because Stewart's conceptual framework also stresses the group interest, or limited pluralism view of representative government. In his dissent in *Lucas,* Stewart attacked the "majoritarianism" commitment of the majority opinion judges. He feared the absolute domination by a geographically concentrated and highly organized majority. (This fear seems to be, based on empirical evidence, a groundless view.[66])

Stewart felt that such a concentrated mass would overwhelm the diverse groups in the state and deny them a representative voice in the political process. In this sense,

Stewart and Clark both were antimajoritarian dissenters. However, Stewart, as did Clark, contrary to the other dissenter—Harlan—did feel that the Equal Protection Clause did prohibit some forms of malapportionment. They both believed in the "crazy quilt" criterion. Stewart maintained that a state's plan had to be rational and also one that would not systematically frustrate the will of the majority (whatever this admonition meant—in the light of his anti-majoritarianism). For reasons already mentioned, the Stewart opinion is also inadequate.

The Harlan opinion has to be distinguished from both the Warren opinion and the Clark–Stewart opinions. While both the majority and the concurring opinions maintained that there was justiciability and jurisdiction and that judicial remedies could be provided where apportionment plans violated the "one man, one vote" or the "crazy quilt" standards, Harlan steadfastly insisted, in the apportionment cases from *Baker* on, that the Courts had no role to play in the apportionment issue. Apportionment was a legislative matter, Harlan maintained, and from no reading of history regarding the Fourteenth Amendment could one possibly infer that that state prohibition amendment had anything to do with the nature and characteristics of state legislative arrangements.

Harlan's conceptual framework, in addition to being anti-majoritarian, stressed the virtues of interest group representation and judicial restraint out of respect for the concept of Federalism. Ironically, his insistence on defending the idea of Federalism as opposed to the idea of judicial intervention ignored the empirical fact that, by intervening in the controversy, the Court was indirectly strengthening the idea of federalism by attempting to strengthen the state legislative structure. Given his con-

ceptual framework, one that differed from Justice Frankfurter in that Frankfurter could and did accept the principle of "majoritarianism" as an ideal characteristic of a
representative democracy but felt that the Courts were
not the appropriate agency to implement this ideal, his
definition of the situation was clear: there was no violation of the Equal Protection Clause and the Supreme
Court's involvement in the issue was an "intolerable interference" by the judiciary into state legislative matters.

His conceptual framework and his definition of the
situation would seem to be inadequate because, based
as they are on non-empirical factors, they ignore reality
and imply that a certain degree of superiority inheres
to certain minority groups who control the machinery of
the state and who disallow majority rule. In this sense,
because his opinions thoroughly deprecate the ideas of
"majoritarianism," "fallibilism," and "open-endedness,"
they are deemed inadequate.

b. The Technical Evaluation and the Justification Phases

Alan Dines, Democratic Speaker of the House of Representatives in the state of Colorado, once commented
on the after-effects of reapportionment. He said that[67]

the new legislature, dominated by urban and suburban
areas, did not discriminate against or punish rural
areas or interests; there simply was no anti-rural coali-
tion. On the contrary, many bills were enacted into
law which were rurally sponsored, rurally supported
and directly aimed at meeting the needs of less populous
counties. . . . On the other and positive side, the 1965
Colorado Legislature did devote a great deal more time
and effort to the consideration of the vast assortment

of existing and emerging urban and suburban problems —problems which previous legislatures, not set up on a "one man, one vote" basis, had sometimes simply ignored, sometimes winked at and shoved under the rug. . . . Reapportionment was not, in and of itself, responsible for this [new] legislation. But to a significant extent, I think, it contributed to all by creating what one might call an atmosphere for action, not inaction, and by breaking up some long-standing, internal legislative alliances which had tended toward inaction.*

These comments are in the way of introducing the technical evaluation phase of the *Reynolds* opinions. Throughout the Warren opinion, the choices perceived were profoundly simple: either protecting constitutional rights or ignoring the appeals of these citizens who had been denied those rights. The consequence, if the petitions were denied, was continued inaction by the state legislatures in the face of new challenges to the states. The consequence, if the Court accepted the controversial issue, according to Warren (and Douglas, Brennan, and Black) , was the description of reality described by Speaker Dines.

Warren's technical evaluation accepted the following premise: "Nothing is more fundamental to representative government—and therefore more constitutional—than the rules governing the electoral process itself."[68] And the rules governing the electoral process—the scheme of ap-

---

* Justice Hugo Black, in an interview with the author, discussed the changes that would take place and said that—regarding Alabama— while changes would be slow, they are present, and reapportioned legislatures based on "one man, one vote" would initiate new relevant state programs that would address themselves to urban poverty issues that had never been broached by malapportioned legislatures. "While changes may be slight," he said, "in the cosmic picture they will ultimately loom large."

portionment—violated the constitution. Data was presented, an awareness of the situational context existed in the Warren opinion, and the Court majority's deliberate handling of issues such as bicameralism, political subdivisions, etc., clearly indicated that the judges were aware of the possible consequences of their choice to enter the "political thicket."

The justification for the entry into the issue of state legislative apportionment was based on the technical evaluation. The reason offered was also a profoundly simple political and legal one: it was the duty of the Court to enter such an issue if the Constitution was at issue. An arbiter had to ensure that the Supremacy Clause controlled any conflict between the Federal Constitution and those of the states; and, since the 1803 *Marbury v. Madison* decision, it has been a standard of political and legal rationality for the Court to engage in such activity. As Chief Justice John Marshall said in that watershed case: "If judges can open it [the Constitution] at all, what part of it are they forbidden to read or obey?"[69] As such, the Court majority acted reasonably and justified its actions on the basis of standards of political rationality.

The short Clark and Stewart opinions in *Reynolds* perceived the Alabama situation in much the same light as did the Warren opinion but their technical evaluation and justifications differed from those of the Chief Justice. The consequences that would follow if the Court incorporated a particular political theory, according to the two justices, would seriously affect the delicate balance between state and federal agencies and jeopardize the role of the Supreme Court.

Their evaluation led them to believe that "equitable remedies" under the Equal Protection Clause were sufficient bases upon which a Court could hear and determine the legality of a state apportionment plan. (Which meant that states would be able to submerge the equal population standard if a plan were rational, or at least was defended as rational state action.) In any event, Clark and Stewart felt that this consequence was better than the consequence that would ensue if states were forced to apportion both houses on the basis of representation.

Their technical evaluation is inadequate for a number of reasons. First of all, they seem to confuse the districting of areas with the apportioning of representatives from these areas to the state legislature. The Warren opinion had indicated that no standards were being established with regard to districting; the constitutional standard was that, based on population, seats should be apportioned to these districts so that equal numbers of people had equal numbers of representatives. If a state wanted, it could maintain traditional political subdivisions—just so long as the population criterion of "one man, one vote" was adhered to in the apportioning of seats.

The Stewart–Clark evaluation is deficient in that the distinctions between the two are blurred. Also, especially in the Stewart dissent in *Lucas,* the fear of majority tyranny is continuously raised. Contrary to Stewart's fear of the tyranny of the urban majority, David Derge has pointed out (among other political scientists commenting on this issue),[70] that "most of the conflict surrounding legislative consideration of urban problems arises from intra-urban disputes, center-city–suburban antagonisms or factionalism within the urban majority."

The justification Clark and Stewart present for their decisions is also inadequate for the following reason: The reasons they present for reaching their conclusion, that "one man, one vote" is an untenable doctrine, are based on an incorrect view of empirical reality and an improper understanding of the dimensions of the standards of legal and political rationality. Although they dissented in two of the cases, *Lucas* and *WMCA v. Lomenzo,* and concurred in the other four (Stewart, however, did not participate in the Maryland case), they did not fully accept the rational premise of the majority opinion, that is, that population must be the fundamental controlling factor in the apportionment of the legislatures—and of both houses of the legislatures.

They reasoned, incorrectly, that the monolithic urban mass would restrain and deny various minority groups access to the political process. They also mistakenly viewed and interpreted the "one man, one vote" standard of the court majority, for they ignored the flexibility that was stressed in the majority opinion regarding districting and the "good faith effort" intention and overlooked the fact that each situation that arose regarding apportionment would be handled on an individual basis—with the "one man" concept used solely as a guide for the judges' (and the legislator's) determinations. For these reasons, the Clark and Stewart decisional choices in the apportionment cases—while superficially agreeing with the majority opinion in some of the cases—seem to be inadequate.

Justice Harlan dissented in every one of the cases that had come before the Court concerning apportionment since 1962. His reasons and his technical evaluations in the nine decisions were basically the same. His perception of choices open to the Courts was the same in every case: either judicial intervention for purposes of interpreting and remaking the Constitution so as to resolve a particular social evil or judicial abstention in a matter that con-

FIGURE SIX

Reynolds v. Sims, 377 US 533

Criteria	Warren Opinion
I. Conceptual Framework	
a. Nature of the Commitment	"Majoritarianism"
b. Objective Sought	Protection of constitutionally protected political rights
c. Adequacy of the definition of the situation	*Adequate.* Empirical perception of the political and social conditions of 20th Century American society.
II. Technical Evaluation	
a. Choices Perceived	Either judicial intervention or continued legislative inaction (unconstitutional).
b. Consequences Perceived	Reaffirmation of democratic faith and democratic institutions given rebirth if Courts act.
c. Adequacy of a. and b.	Adequate. Perceptions of consequences, and of the situation, realistic.
d. Structure of the Opinion	Organized, but cumbersome.
III. Terms of the Justification	
a. Good reasons offered?	*Yes.*
b. Is there an adequate justification?	*Yes.* Standards of political and judicial rationality followed.
IV. Overall Evaluation of Opinion	*Reasonable opinion.*

Clark-Stewart Opinions

Criteria

I. Conceptual Framework

a. Nature of the Commitment	"Group Representation"
b. Objective Sought	Protection (crazy quilt criterion) of groups against arbitrary action.
c. Adequacy of the definition of the situation	*Inadequate.* Cannot perceive empirical restrictions on majority rule principle.

II. Technical Evaluation

a. Choices Perceived	Judicial action only when "crazy quilt" pattern exists; otherwise states need not be restricted by "one man" doctrine.
b. Consequences Perceived	If "one man" applied, stifling effect on state legislatures.
c. Adequacy of a. and b.	*Inadequate.* Not realistic.
d. Structure of the Opinion	Errors of fact and philosophy in re: representative government.

III. Terms of the Justification

a. Good reasons offered?	*No.*
b. Is there an adequate justification?	*No.* Standards of Rationality not followed.
IV. Overall Evaluation of Opinion	No good reasons presented.

Harlan Opinion

Criteria

I. *Conceptual Framework*

    a. Nature of the Commitment   "Judicial Restraint"

    a. Objective Sought   Preservation of judicial integrity; maintain inviolability of state legislative actions.

    c. Adequacy of the definition of the situation   *Inadequate.* Ignores empirical events that block access to political process of certain groups.

II. *Technical Evaluation*

    a. Choices Perceived   Judicial meddling into legislative activities; judicial restraint and maintenance of Federal system.

    b. Consequences Perceived   Fabric of federalism weakened.

    c. Adequacy of a. and b.   *Inadequate.* Not realistic. Based on elitist political philosophy.

    d. Structure of the Opinion   Errors of fact and philosophy in re: representative government.

III. *Terms of the Justification*

    a. Good reasons offered?   *No.*

    b. Is there an adequate justification?   *No.* Standards of rationality not followed.

IV. *Overall Evaluation of Opinion*   No good reasons presented.

cerned the legislative branch only. The consequences that would follow from judicial intervention would be disastrous for the system; they would sap the body politics; they would weaken the "fabric of federalism"; they would encourage "popular inertia" and thereby greatly weaken the political process.

But as of this time, as already pointed out in this and other chapters, the political process has not been weakened; it has, instead, been reactivated. Since the Court entered the controversy, 46 of the 50 states have apportioned themselves in line with the "one man, one vote" doctrine. Interesting political questions have arisen since the Court's decisions regarding the nature, purpose, and extent of representative government, that is, a dialogue has opened up on the very essence of democracy. In November 1966, the Louis Harris poll indicated that the reapportionment decisions received the highest rate of approval—76 percent—of those citizens interviewed.[71]

Far from impairing the nature of the American political process, most observers would say that the Court decisions prodded the political leaders of the society into reappraising their commitments to representative government and democracy. Certainly, then, one can say that the Harlan technical evaluation is inadequate in that it ignores reality—political and social changes that have taken place since *Baker v. Carr.*

The justification for Harlan's choice in these cases is also inadequate. It is inadequate partly because it is based on improper and incorrect reasons; it is inadequate because it ignores standards of political and legal rationality in the matter of judicial intervention in cases involving the violation of constitutionally protected rights. He justifies his action on the basis of an elitist, anti-majoritarian normative commitment to interest group representation. Such a stand ignores the contrary principles of representative government and democracy to which this country is committed.

III. POST-REYNOLDS QUESTIONS AND JUDICIAL SOLUTIONS

The Supreme Court had reached a plateau with the announcement of the *Reynolds* decision. A general constitutional principle had been established regarding national and state reapportionment. Over a succeeding five-year period, through the 1968 term of the Court, the justices did begin to "develop a body of doctrine on a case-by-case basis."[72] Some constitutional tests, quite precise, were spelled out by the Supreme Court in response to three basic unsettled questions:

(1) What was the constitutional position of multi-member, floterial, and single member districts, or combinations of these types of districts? And what about the constitutionality of apportionment plans that excluded certain categories of citizens when drawn up?

(2) Was there to be a total extension of the "one man" standard to city councils, school board representation, county organization, and other political subdivisions?

(3) If "Mathematical Exactness" was an impossible standard for legislatures to follow when apportioning, what degree of mathematical deviation from the "ideal" population standard was permissible?

The following sections of this chapter will present, in brief, the opinions of the Supreme Court that sought "the most satisfactory means of arriving at detailed constitutional requirements in the area of state legislative reapportionment."[73] As will be noted in the concluding chapter, there is a basic division of opinion in the succeeding, post-Reynolds, opinions. In the discussion of the unresolved problems, a presentation of all the views will be made. A concluding section will summarize and evaluate these post-Reynolds reapportionment opinions.

a. Nature and Variety of Representational Districts and the Constitutionality of Certain "Measures of Population"

In *Fortson v. Dorsey*, a 1965 Georgia case,[74] and, the following year, in the *Burns v. Richardson*[75] (Hawaii) reapportionment case, the Supreme Court majority (in opinions written by Justice William J. Brennan, Jr.) addressed itself to two questions: (1) permissible types of reapportionment schemes, and (2) state measures of "population."

The Georgia case involved an apportionment statute that allocated 54 senatorial seats among 54 senatorial districts. These districts were to be drawn so far as possible along existing Georgia county lines, that is, in accordance with the "one vote" principle expressed in *Reynolds*. (There are 159 counties in Georgia.) The statute did offer certain discriminations, however, and these were to be the basis for the litigation proceedings that culminated in the *Fortson* decision in 1965.

The statutory discrimination was as follows: where there was more than one senatorial district located in a county, all that county's senators had to be elected by an at-large county-wide vote. As it turned out, there were 33 single-member senatorial districts and these were made up of from one to eight counties each (152 of the 159

Georgia counties had district-wide voting schemes). The rest of the senatorial districts, 21, were multi-member districts, with from two to seven senatorial districts allocated to each of the remaining seven (most populous) counties—with the subsequent county-wide, at-large election.

The constitutional complaint, based on this discrimination, was that the statute, by requiring some senators to reside in a district within the large counties "while his tenure depends on a county-wide electorate," thus dilutes the weight of the vote "of the people in his home district."[76] The federal District Court ruling declared that the statute did violate the equal protection clause of the Fourteenth Amendment and that it was therefore null and void.

On appeal to the Supreme Court, however, Justice Brennan stated that absent any contention that (1) there was not substantial equality of population among the districts or (2) evidence, facts, to support the assertion that the statute was intended "to minimize or cancel out the voting strength of racial or political elements of the voting population," the statute was constitutional:[77] Brennan specifically rejected the notion that (1) the equal protection clause necessarily requires the formation of single-member districts: "Whatever the means of accomplishment, the overriding objective must be substantial equality of population among the various districts, so that the vote of any citizen is approximately equal in weight to any other citizen in the state." And (2) indicated that the data did not show any mathematical disparity between the county-wide and the district-wide vote.[78]

Justice William O. Douglas, Jr. was the sole dissenter

in the *Fortson* case. He argued that there was an "invidious discrimination" evident because the apportionment statute violated the Georgia state constitution's apportionment directions. The Constitution makes "Senatorial District" the sole unit in the election of senators. The Reapportionment Act develops two classifications: Senatorial Districts (a) comprising more than one county, (b) comprising less than one county (where voters must share the choice of senators with other electors in their county). It is an invidious discrimination, reasoned Douglas, because the voters are treated differently; "some are allowed to select their representatives based on homesite, others are not."[79]

The following year, in the Hawaii case, *Burns v. Richardson,* the Supreme Court upheld the use of multi-member districts, largely on the basis of the *Fortson* opinion. Hawaii's legislative plan had been disputed by a three-judge Federal District Court, which claimed that the plan, instead of using single-member district voting, called for the election of all senators at large from multi-member districts.

Brennan's opinion indicated that, in the absence of evidence that such an apportionment plan limited the activities of racial or political minorities, the use of multi-member districts did not constitute invidious discrimination in violation of the fourteenth amendment's equal protection clause. "Equal protection does not require at least one house to have single-member district representation."[80]

The second substantive question raised in *Burns* concerned the fact that Hawaii had based its Senate reapportionment on the basis of numbers of "registered voters" rather than on numbers of "actual voters." For the Court (there were no dissenters; Justices Harlan and Stewart concurred and Justice Fortas did not participate because his former law firm had represented Hawaii's Governor, John A. Burns, in the litigation proceedings), this was a critical issue, and Brennan's remarks reflected their concern.

He pointed out that none of the Supreme Court's reapportionment opinions suggested to the states that they be required to include aliens, (military) transients, short term or temporary residents, or persons denied the vote for conviction of crime in the apportionment base by which their legislators are distributed or against which compliance with the Equal Protection clause is to be measured.[81]

Yet it is possible, indicated Brennan, for a state to develop a plan—such as the type Hawaii adopted; that is, the "registered voter" plan—that would "be used to perpetuate underrepresentation of groups constitutionally entitled to participate in the political process, or perpetuate a ghost of prior malapportionment."[82] Therefore, the Court has to examine each plan on its merits, viewing the data presented by litigants and available independently, in order to determine if invidious discrimination is present.

In the Hawaii case, the Court held "that the present reapportionment satisfies the Equal Protection clause *only* because on this record it was found to have produced a distribution of legislators not substantially different from that which would have resulted from the use of a permissible population basis."[83] (The Court opinion indicated that Oahu, the largest of the Hawaiian Islands with a 1960 population of 500,409, had 79 percent of the total population and elected 76 percent of the senatorial representatives—19 of 25 senatorial seats—and elected 71 percent of the house seats—36 of 51 seats.) [84] Brennan did end his opinion with a discreet warning: "We are not to be understood as deciding that the validity of the registered voter basis as a measure has been established for all time or circumstances."[85]

The Court, in *Burns* and *Fortson*, was saying that various patterns of districting and various "population" measures may be used, so long as there was no indication, on its face, of invidious discrimination based on race, class, or homesite. In both decisions, the Court was indicating a "willingness to defer to the wishes of state legislatures whenever possible, including cases in which harm to certain groups was anticipated but not proved."[86] (It may very well be that, in the future, when harm to "minorities living in concentrated neighborhoods or ghettoes" is perceived by judges as "proved," that the Supreme Court, in this future instance, may "insist on the subdistricting of multi-member districts.")[87]

b. The Extent to Which the "One Man" Principle Is to Be Applied to Local Political Subdivisions

In a trio of cases handed down in the 1966 and 1967 terms, the Supreme Court extended the "reapportionment revolution"[88] almost totally to all local units of state government. These were *Sailors v. Board of Education of the County of Kent, Michigan*,[89] *Dusch v. Davis*,[90] and, most important, *Avery v. Midland County, Texas*.[91]

Sailors and *Dusch*, handed down the same day, involved, respectively, the legality of Michigan county school boards and the constitutionality of a representational plan under which local councilmen were elected in Virginia Beach,

Virginia. In Michigan, county school boards were chosen by delegates from the local school boards. These delegates chose from candidates who were nominated by school electors, and not by the electors of the county. The claim made, and rejected by the three-judge District Court—and the Supreme Court—was that the plan violated the Equal Protection clause of the Constitution.

Douglas, writing the opinion of the Court in *Sailors,* indicated that there was "no constitutional reason why state or local officers of the nonlegislative character involved here may not be chosen by the governor, by the legislature, or by some other appointive means rather than by an election."[92] Members of a school board, the Court went on, which was "not legislative in the classical sense" (board membership was "basically appointive rather than elective") , need not come from districts which were equal in population. "We see nothing in the Constitution to prevent experimentation," Douglas said, and "since the choice of members of the county school board did not involve an election and since none was required for these nonlegislative offices, the principle of 'one man, one vote' has no relevancy."[93] Furthermore, he concluded, the Court is aware that "viable local governments may need many innovations, numerous combinations of old and new devices, great flexibility in municipal arrangements to meet changing urban conditions."[94]

This flexible attitude evidenced itself once again in the second case concerning the extension of the "one man" doctrine to local political subdivisions. In *Dusch v. Davis,* the Supreme Court had to determine whether a local government consolidation "7–4" plan was consistent with the one man, one vote principle. Virginia Beach, Virginia, a tourist area, was consolidated within Princess Anne

County (which contained three rural and three urban boroughs), to form a local government unit of seven boroughs which varied considerably in population.

Under the "7–4" Plan, the city council was to consist of eleven members, each elected at-large. Four would be chosen without regard to residency, the other seven had to reside in each of the seven different boroughs. While the District Court approved of this consolidation plan, the Court of Appeals reversed the decision: it felt that *Reynolds* required "each legislator to represent a reasonably like number in population"[95] and that the plan violated the "one man, one vote" principle (it pointed out that Blackwater borough had 733 voters and had the same representation as did Lynnhaven with 23,731 voters).

Justice William Douglas, Jr., writing for the Court in *Dusch*, overruled the Court of Appeals reversal. In the eyes of the Supreme Court justices, the 7–4 Plan "makes no distinction on the basis of race, creed, or economic status or location."[96] The fact that seven of the eleven must reside in one of the seven boroughs "is not fatal. It is merely a residency requirement; it is not a basis for voting or representation."[97] He concluded by stating that the plan "seems to reflect a detente between urban and rural communities that may be important in resolving the complex problems of the modern megalopolis in relation to the city, suburbia and the rural countryside. Finding no invidious discrimination, the Court of Appeals judgment is reversed."[98]

A year later, in the 1967 case of *Avery v. Midland County, Texas,* the Supreme Court extended the "one man, one vote" principle to include prescriptions regarding the election of local government officials similar to those announced in the *Reynolds* case for the election of state officials. The Texas State Constitution established governing bodies for the counties in the state. The Midland County Commissioner's Court was one such state constitutional creation consisting of five members: a county judge (elected at-large), and four commissioners, one elected from each of the four districts (precincts) into which the County is divided. (The county had a total population of about 70,000—67,906 citizens living within the Midland City district, with 852, 414, and 828 citizens living in the other three districts.)

Under the Constitution, the Commissioner's Court was the governing body of the county and it held and exercised such broad governmental functions as budget setting, development of public housing for the county, school construction, setting of tax rates, assessments, fixing of school district boundaries, etc.

In the state courts, the appellants claimed that the gross disparity in population distribution among the four districts violated the Equal Protection clause of the Fourteenth Amendment and the "one man, one vote" principle established by *Reynolds*. The Texas Supreme Court upheld the plan on appeal and the case went to the Supreme Court for decision. To Justice Byron White, writing for the Supreme Court, the basic question was this: Does the Fourteenth Amendment forbid election of local government officials from districts of disparate population? The Court's answer, provoking bitter dissenting opinions from Justices Fortas, Harlan, and Stewart, was: Yes, such discrimination in apportionment is invidious and in opposition to the Constitution of the United States.

Noting that the highest state courts in eight states and four District Courts had already applied the *Reynolds* principle to units of local government,[99] White maintained that "it is beyond question that a state's political subdivisions must comply with the Fourteenth Amendment:"[100]

The actions of local government *are* the actions of the state.

> A city, town, or county may no more deny equal protection of the laws than it may abridge freedom of speech, establish an official religion, arrest without probable cause, or deny due process of law.

When delegating lawmaking powers to local government and when providing for the election of local officials, the state "must insure that those qualified to vote have the right to an equally effective voice in the election process."[101]

The majority opinion asserted that the Commissioner's Courts were assigned legislative, administrative, executive and judicial tasks, and that these were "representative of the tasks given most general governing bodies of American cities, counties, towns and villages."[102] The Court makes decisions for all the residents (or, as White maintained, makes decisions "not to exercise a function within the Court's power, for example, not to build an airport or a library, or not to participate in the Federal foodstamp program"[103]).

The Supreme Court majority opinion further stated that only "special purpose units of government, assigned the performance of functions affecting definable groups of constituents more than other constituents,"[104] would possibly fall outside the scope of the "one man" principle: "We would have to confront the question whether such a [special purpose] body may be apportioned in ways which give greater influence to the citizens most affected by the organization's functions."[105] The Commissioner's Court, however, was a "general purpose" body and, as such, subject to the "one man, one vote" principle.

White went out of his way to defend the Court's action. *Sailors* and *Dusch,* he indicated, "demonstrate that the Constitution and this Court are not roadblocks in the path of innovation, experiment and development among units of local government."[106] The Court will not bar the emergence of new structures of public bodies, "equipped with new capacities and motivations."[107] What the Court majority did bar, by applying "one man, one vote" to local subdivisions of a state, was a state of affairs where units of government, with general governmental powers, were apportioned in such a manner so as to disregard the principle of political equality.

The dissenters, Harlan, Stewart, and Fortas, disagreed with the majority opinion on its merits. All argued that it was irresponsible for the Court to extend the "one man, one vote" principle to over 80,000 units of local government. Fortas's criticisms were particularly acute: "Constitutional commands are not surgical instruments. They have a tendency to hack deeply—to amputate. And while I have no doubt that, with the growth of suburbia and exurbia, the problem of allocating local government functions and benefits urgently requires attention, I am persuaded that it does not require the hatchet of one man, one vote."[108]

All argued that a more flexible approach was needed to the complex problems of local government and that the application of the *Reynolds* principle reflected "the arithmetic simplicity of one equals one."[109] (Additionally, an important note, Fortas did disagree with the majority's notion that the Commissioner's Court was a general purpose unit of local government: "the Commissioners see themselves only as road commissioners . . . there is an absence of chief executive and a diffusion of responsibility which is a major characteristic of county government," etc.) [110]

The majority, in this trio of cases, distinguished between "special purpose" units (such as school boards) and "general purpose" units of local government (the Texas Commissioner's Courts), the former not having to follow the dictates of the "one man" standard, while the latter, after Avery, had to conform to the Reynolds principle of political equality.

c. The Question of Mathematical Deviations from the Population Ideal

Another question that was raised after the Reynolds decision was handed down was this: would the Court identify a precise range of deviation from a (practically impossible) absolute numerical equality that was allowable under the one man, one vote principle? In two recent cases, handed down in the 1967 and the 1968 terms, Swann v. Adams, [111] and Kirkpatrick v. Preisler, [112] the Supreme Court majority maintained that burden was on the state to defend deviations from population by showing (1) unavoidability of deviations despite a "good faith" attempt or by (2) justifying the non-discriminatory and minor deviations by being able to articulate acceptable "justifiable" reasons for them.

It may well be that the answer to this question, one that was fully developed in these recent cases, was born in the 1964 reapportionment decision, Roman v. Sincock. [113] In that opinion, the Court had said that the proper judicial approach was to determine whether in the particular state "there has been a faithful adherence to a plan of population-based representation, with such minor deviations only as may occur in recognizing certain factors that are free from any taint of arbitrariness or discrimination."[114]

In *Swann*, a Florida case, the state legislature had set up a new legislative apportionment plan (after *Reynolds*). It provided for 48 Senators and 117 Representatives. However, the Senate deviation ranged from 15.09% above the average to 10.56% below and House deviations ranged from 18.28% overrepresentation to 15.27% underrepresentation. The Supreme Court, for the third time, turned back to Florida reapportionment law because "the State does not present any acceptable reasons for population variances between districts."[115] For this reason, lack of justification for the state policy, the Court invalidated the plan. In dicta, referring to interstate comparisons, Justice Byron White indicated that "variation from the norm approved in one state has little relevance to the validity of a similar variation in another state."[116]

In his dissent, Justice Harlan (joined by Justice Potter Stewart) argued that the burden of proof should fall on the shoulders of the attacking party and that the attacking party "has not proved his case" by not being able to show an invidious discrimination.[117]

In its most recent pronouncement, involving a 1967 Missouri congressional reapportionment statute, the Supreme Court, in the *Kirkpatrick v. Preisler* opinion written by Justice Brennan in 1968, declared that, because of maximum deviations of 2.83% underrepresentation and 3.13% overrepresentation, the plan did not meet the Federal constitutional requirement that, as nearly as practicable, there should be population equality. As Brennan stated, the case required the Court "to elucidate the 'as nearly as practicable' standard announced in Wesberry" (this was a congressional redistricting case).[118]

In deciding against the statute, the Brennan opinion upheld the District Court judgment. The District Court had found that (1) the Missouri legislators did not use accurate census data, (2) the legislators had rejected a plan that would have produced even smaller variances, (3) switching some counties from one district to another would have produced a plan with markedly reduced variances among the districts.[119] This was to be an important factor in the opinion of the majority. The judicial test, from Wesberry through and beyond Reynolds, was that "as nearly as practicable" the state make a "good faith" attempt to achieve precise mathematical equality. And, the second test, "Unless population variances among congressional districts are shown to have resulted despite such effort, the state must justify each variance, no matter how small."[120]

That the task was complex the Court's majority opinion admitted: "the extent to which equality may practically be achieved may differ from state to state and from district to district."[121] The Court, however, would not "pick a cutoff point at which population variances suddenly become de minimus. Moreover, [to do this] would encourage legislatures to strive for that range rather than for equality as nearly as practicable."[122]

Based on the data supplied to the Courts, Brennan's opinion concluded that the variances were not unavoidable and that there was no state justification for these deviations. The Court could not accept, therefore, the Missouri apportionment plan as it stood.

Harlan's dissent, joined in by Justice Stewart, was a bitter one. He chastised the Court's "Draconian judgments" that have turned "a political slogan (*Reynolds*) into a constitutional absolute,"[123] and utterly rejected the idea that "the constitution requires that mathematics be a substitute for common sense in the art of statecraft."[123] Justice White also dissented, saying that the Court's ruling "is an unduly rigid and unwarranted application of the Equal Protection clause which will unnecessarily involve the Courts in the abrasive task of drawing district lines."[125]

In this special area—deviations from the ideal of political-population equality—the Court majority has suggested that the decision rests with the particular situations surrounding each controversy. In particular, the Court seems to be looking for "good faith" attempts by the state and/or acceptable justifications for minor deviations from the "one man, one vote" standard.

d. The Unanswered Question: Gerrymandered Districts

Gerrymandering is a substantive question associated with the apportionment controversy of the last decade, but one that goes back in time to the eighteenth century in England and in early America. Present the gerrymandered district and perfect equality of population from district to district may be irrelevant insofar as the nature of and types of legislators one gets from these gerrymandered boundaries. There have been only two major cases that have come to the Supreme Court regarding the gerrymander and the apportionment process. Both involved racial minorities and both were decided before the 1964 *Reynolds* opinion was pronounced. These were *Gomil-*

lion v. Lightfoot (1958),[126] and *Wright v. Rockefeller* (1964).[127]

The *Gomillion* case involved a Tuskegee, Alabama, redistricting plan that virtually excluded from the city all but four or five of the city's 400 black voters. Treating it as a voting rights case, under the jurisdiction of the 15th Amendment, Justice Frankfurter struck the reapportionment plan down as a patent state attempt to impair the voting rights guarantees contained in the Federal constitution.[128]

In the second case, involving a New York congressional plan that created an almost all-white congressional district next to a predominantly black district *(Wright v. Rockefeller)*, the Court majority maintained that there was a failure to show "state contrivance" to segregate on the basis of race or place of origin and that, if anything, there was de facto segregation in that high concentrations of Puerto Rican and black voters "made it impossible, even assuming that to be permissible, to approximate an equal division of these groups among the districts.[129] In strong dissents, Justices Douglas and Goldberg argued that there was racial gerrymandering present and, in the words of Justice Douglas, " 'Separate but equal' and 'separate but better off' have no more place in voting districts than they have in schools, parks, railroad terminals, or any other facility serving the public."[130]

To date, the Court has not heard other cases concerning reapportionment and gerrymandering. This is not to say that the problem does not exist. It does, and if, in the future, the Court does listen, in litigation proceedings, to the question of the gerrymander, it will certainly be at the very dead center of the "political thicket."

e. Summary and Evaluation

With the exception of the substantive gerrymander issue, the Supreme Court, since the *Reynolds* decision, has shown a great deal of flexibility in responding to the critical, second generation, reapportionment problems. Overall, the judicial actions did not demonstrate road-block action "in the path of innovation, experiment, and development."

The three unsettled questions were handled equitably by the Supreme Court. The basic criterion for acceptability of the various apportionment plans (given the "one man" standard) was a fair and empirical question: was there indicated a "good faith" attempt by the state legislators to meet the basic requirements of the Constitution?

Another important decision by the Court during this time was to review all the reapportionment cases on their merits—instead of handling these important issues summarily via the *per curiam* decision route. As was indicated in the Missouri case, *Kirkpatrick v. Preisler,* variations that take place in apportionment plans may be constitutionally permissible—given the uniqueness of the state situation under investigation. As such, based on the "one man, one vote" and the "as nearly as practicable" standards, reapportionment cases have to be examined—empirically—individually. The actions of legislators, accordingly, will have to be judged individually, with the Court examining their attempts to reapportion fairly and/or the legislators' reasons for justifying the minor inequities in their plans.

In sum, the Court did act fairly because it did examine, by raising empirical questions, the issues in each of the state cases. "One man, one vote," like other constitutional standards, has become a device used by the judges to determine whether or not states and legislators have acted reasonably and fairly or whether they have "invidiously" discriminated. *Reynolds* added something to the makeup of the democratic credo, which is really a set of vague symbols existing at a high level of abstraction. The post-Reynolds cases offer an extended example of the credo becoming reality.

NOTES: CHAPTER FIVE

1. *Wesberry v Sanders,* 376 *US* 1 (1964) , at 7.
2. *Id.* at 8–9.
3. *Id.* at 18.
4. *Id.* at 20.
5. *Id.* at 48.
6. G. Theodore Mitau, *Decade of Decision,* New York, Scribner's & Sons, 1967, p. 95.
7. *Reynolds v Sims,* 377 *US* 533 (1964) , at 560–561.
8. *Id.* at 561.
9. Glendon Schubert, *Judicial Policy-Making,* p. 135.
10. *Id.,* passim, pp. 537–554.
11. *The New York Times,* June 16, 1964, page 38.
12. *Reynolds,* at 554.
13. *Id.* at 555.
14. *Id.* at 562.
15. *Id.* at 565.
16. *Id.*
17. *Id.*
18. *Id.* at 562.
19. *Id.* at 563.
20. *Id.* at 567.
21. *Id.*
22. *Id.* at 567–568.
23. *Id.* at 569.
24. *Id.* at 566.

25. *Id.* at 577.
26. *Id.*
27. *Id.* at 568.
28. *Id.* at 564.
29. *Id.* at 569.
30. *Id.* at 568, see footnote 45.
31. *Id.* at 567, see footnote 43 at 556.
32. *Id.* at 563.
33. *Id.* at 562.
34. *Id.* at 566.
35. *Id.* at 573.
36. *Id.* at 576.
37. *Id.* at 583.
38. *Id.* at 578.
39. *Id.* at 566.
40. *Id.* at 576.
41. *Id.* at 587.
42. *Id.* at 584.
43. *Id.*
44. Associate Justice Arthur Goldberg, "Gideon's Trumpet," *op cit.*, p. 27.
45. *Reynolds,* at 588.
46. *Id.*
47. *Id.* at 587.
48. *Lucas v 44th General Assembly of Colorado,* 377 *US* 713, at 753–754.
49. *Id.* at 754.
50. *Id.* at 748.
51. *Reynolds v Sims,* 12 *L Ed 2d* 506, at 544.
52. *Id.*
53. *Id.,* passim, pp. 545–558.
54. *Id.* at 559–560.
55. *Id.* at 561.
56. *Id.* at 561–563.
57. *Id.* at 563.
58. *Id.*
59. See, for example, A. Spencer Hill, "The Reapportionment Decisions: A Return to Dogma?," 31 *Journal of Politics,* Feb. 1969, p. 186.
60. Hanson, *op cit.,* p. 79.
61. See *Sailors v Kent Board of Education,* 387 *US* D5, 1967.
62. *Reynolds,* at 578.
63. Auerbach, *op cit.,* p. 67.
64. *Lucas,* at 724.
65. Jewell, *op cit.,* p. 8.
66. See, Auerbach, *op cit.,* pp. 49–53, especially.

67. Alan Dines, "A Reapportioned State," 55 *National Municipal Review*, No. 2, February 1966, pp. 70–74, at 74.
68. Auerbach, *op cit.*, pp. 66–67.
69. *Marbury v Madison*, 1 *Cranch* 137, 1803.
70. David Derge, "Urban Rural Conflict: The Case In Illinois," in H. Wahlke and H. Eulau, editors, *Legislative Behavior: A Reader in Theory and Research*, Glencoe, The Free Press, Inc., 1959.
71. As quoted in G. Theodore Mitau, *Decade of Decision: The Supreme Court and the Constitutional Revolution, 1954–1964*, New York, Charles Scribner's and Sons, 1967, pp. 5–7.
72. *Reynolds*, at 578.
73. *Id.*
74. 379 *US* 433 (1965).
75. 384 *US* 73 (1966).
76. 379 *US* 433, 436.
77. *Id.*
78. *Id.* at 437.
79. *Id.* at 441.
80. 384 *US* 73, 86.
81. *Id.* at 92.
82. *Id.* at 92–93.
83. *Id.* at 93.
84. *Id.* at 81.
85. *Id.* at 93.
86. *New York Times*, April 26, 1966, p. 15.
87. Mitau, *op cit.*, p. 97.
88. See, generally, Gordon Baker, *The Reapportionment Revolution*.
89. 387 *US* 105 (1966).
90. 387 *US* 12 (1966).
91. 390 *US* 474 (1967).
92. 387 *US* 105, 108.
93. *Id.* at 111.
94. *Id.* at 110–111.
95. 387 *US* 112, 114.
96. *Id.* at 116.
97. *Id.* at 115.
98. *Id.* at 117.
99. 390 *US* 474, 479.
100. *Id.* at 480.
101. *Id.*
102. *Id.* at 482.
103. *Id.* at 484.
104. *Id.* at 483–484.

105. *Id.* at 484.
106. *Id.* at 485.
107. *Id.*
108. *Id.* at 497.
109. *Id.* at 496.
110. *Id.* at 500–503.
111. 385 *US* 440 (1967).
112. 22 *L Ed 2d* 519 (1968).
113. 377 *US* 695 (1964).
114. *Id.* at 699.
115. 385 *US* 440, 443.
116. *Id.* at 445.
117. *Id.* at 447–448.
118. 22 *L Ed 2d* 519, 520.
119. *Id.* at 520–521.
120. *Id.* at 524.
121. *Id.*
122. *Id.* at 525.
123. *Id.* at 530–531.
124. *Id.* at 532.
125. *Id.* at 533.
126. 364 *US* 339 (1958).
127. 376 *US* 52 (1963).
128. 364 *US* 339, 340.
129. 376 *US* 52, 55.
130. *Id.* at 67.

6

The Supreme Court's Role
in the Maintenance
of the Society's Commitment
to the Principles
of Democracy and Equal
Representation

INTRODUCTION

The focus of this investigation of the Supreme Court's apportionment opinions has been to identify the conceptions of democracy held by the various judges and to determine whether or not one group of these opinions could be judged reasonable. The opening statement set the tone of the study: by establishing a new constitutional standard of "'one man, one vote," the Supreme Court established new legal and political relationships; in so doing did the Court act reasonably? This chapter will sum up the judgments made in the body of the investigation;

it will suggest that the Court majority did act reasonably primarily because it protected, enforced, and generally maintained the basic societal symbols—democracy, representative government, and political equality—in an era of rapid change.

This Chapter will discuss, in turn, (1) the intense consistency of the four basic judicial attitudes and theoretical conceptions of Democracy and of Representative Government that have appeared in the reapportionment cases; (2) The reasons why the Supreme Court majorities in *Baker, Grey, Reynolds,* and the post-*Reynolds* cases are judged to have acted rationally with regard to the issue of apportionment; and (3) The seldom used but important role of the Supreme Court in an age that evidences "crises in values"; judicial superimposition of democratic promises and ideals over democratic reality. There will also be some closing comments on the nature and the problems of evaluating Supreme Court decisions.

I. FOUR BASIC JUDICIAL ATTITUDES

Using scale analysis, "which measures the presence of a single dominant variable in a set of additional data" by "providing a technique for arranging the [several related] cases [decided on the merits by the Court] and the respondent judges in uniquely determined rank orders," and which "can tell us both how consistent and how intense the underlying-attitudes of the respective individual justices" have been,[1] one immediately notices, in the apportionment cases, an extremely high degree of attitudinal consistency and intensity. As seen in Figure Seven,

Scalogram of the Apportionment Cases, 1962–1968, "scale analysis [has] traced the existence of this consistency by organizing the behavioral data on the population under examination."[2]

In the scaling process, only two errors, that is, non-scale judicial responses (of Justice White in *Avery* and Justice Stewart in *Swann*), developed out of a total of 113 judicial responses. What one perceives, when examining the results of the analysis, is a number of patterns of behavior, four in all, with regard to the reapportionment issue. Judges identified with these patterns are (1) the Douglas-Goldberg and the (2) Warren-Black-Brennan-Marshall-White, and (marginally) Fortas groupings, who have been referred to in the previous chapters as the "majoritarians"; (3) the Clark-Stewart and the (4) Frankfurter-Harlan groupings, both differing with the Court "majoritarians" yet both distinguishable in their own right.

Essentially, four political theories of democracy and representative government were expressed by the justices in these cases through 1968. In the four views, one of two assertions regarding the role and function of the Supreme Court was also present and was a major aspect accounting for the justices' attitudes toward representative government: (1) *judicial activism,* that is, that Courts "ought not to be impotent" in the face of state actions clearly violative of the Constitutional commands, and (2) *judicial restraint,* that is, that the remedy for unfairness (if it, indeed, exists in these cases) lies not with the Courts but with the people and the legislatures and that, contrary to the judicial activists, judicial interference into such a political controversy, would "weaken the fabric of federalism."

FIGURE SEVEN. *Scalogram of the Apportionment Cases, 1962–1968*

Case: Justices	Wesberry, 1964	Grey, 1963	Reynolds, 1964	Swann, 1967	Baker, 1962	Lucas, 1964	Kirkpatrick, 1968	Avery, 1967	Wright, 1964	Fortson, 1965	Burns, 1966	Sailors, 1967	Dusch, 1967	Total Number, Votes Cast, Per Justice	Total Number of Inconsistencies
Douglas	+	(+)	+	+	+	+	+	+	+	+	−	(−)	(−)	13	0
Goldberg	+	+	+	⊕	⊕	+	⊕	⊕	+	⊕	⊖	⊖	⊖	5	0
Warren	+	+	(+)	+	+	(+)	+	+	−	−	−	−	−	13	0
Black	(+)	+	+	+	+	+	+	+	(−)	−	−	−	−	13	0
Brennan	+	+	+	+	(+)	+	+	(+)	−	(−)	(−)	−	−	13	0
Marshall	⊕	⊕	⊕	⊕	⊕	⊕	+	⊕*	⊖	⊖	⊖	⊖	⊖	1	0
Fortas	⊕	⊕	⊕	+	⊕	⊕	+	−	⊖	−	⊖*	−	−	6	0
White	+	+	+	(+)	⊕	+	−	(+)	−	−	−	−	−	11	1
Clark	+	+	+	+	+	−	⊖	⊖	−	−	−	−	−	11	0
Stewart	+	+	+	−	+	−	−	−	−	.−	−	−	−	13	1
Harlan	−	−	−	−	−	−	−	−	−	−	−	−	−	13	0
Frankfurter	⊖	⊖	⊖	⊖	−	⊖	⊖	⊖	⊖	⊖	⊖	⊖	⊖	1	0
Total:	9	9	9	9	8	9	9	8	9	9	8	9	9	113	2
Division + of Votes	8	8	8	7	6	6	6	5	2	1	0	0	0	$CR = 1 - (\frac{e}{r})$	
−	1	1	1	2	2	3	3	3	7	8	9	9	9	$CR = .982$	

Legend: + = Acceptance of argument that apportionment was unconstitutional
 − = Rejection of argument
 ( ) = Wrote opinion
 O = Not on Court at time
 * = On Court, did not participate

a. "Majoritarianism: Judicial Activism"

The two "majoritarianism" views of representative government, held by Justices Douglas, Goldberg, Brennan, Black, and by Warren, White, Marshall, and Fortas (with the exception of the *Avery* decision) was summed up by the Chief Justice in his *Reynolds* opinion. He said that "representative government is, in essence, self-government through the medium of elected representatives of the people" and that "logically, in a society grounded on representative government, it would seem reasonable that a majority of the people of a state could elect a majority of that state's legislators. To conclude differently, and to sanction minority control of state legislative bodies, would appear to deny majority rights in a way that far surpasses any possible denial of minority rights that might otherwise be thought to result." Political equality, the "mainspring of representative government," meant, to these justices, "one man, one vote." There must be equal weight and equal representation for equal numbers of people said, implicitly and explicitly, the majority opinions since *Baker* (and Black's minority opinion in *Colegrove*).

Justices Goldberg and Douglas did differ from the remaining members of the "majoritarian" clique. Both sided with the individuals bringing suit against the New York Congressional districting plan that was alleged to be, partially, racially gerrymandered (i.e., the Wright v. Rockefeller case in 1964). Justice Douglas was the sole dissenter in a case decided during the 1965 term (Goldberg was no longer on the Court) concerning a Georgia reapportionment case. He maintained that the state statute was an "invidious discrimination." It is Douglas's actions in these two cases that separate him from the others. Perhaps he should be called an "egalitarian majoritarian."*

Within such a conceptual framework of democracy and representative government, the courts play a vital role in maintaining vital rights such as voting equality; suffrage rights must not be impaired by state action. If there is an impairment or blockage of this basic democratic right, then it is the duty and obligation of the courts to intervene and resolve the dispute. The role of the courts in the American federal system, according to both groupings of "majoritarians," became an integral part of their political philosophy of representative government. In a sense, the "majoritarian" justices accepted Chief Justice John Marshall's admonition in *McCulloch v Maryland*:

> No tribunal can approach such a question (Federal laws and contradictory state actions) without a deep sense of its importance and of the awful responsibility in its decision. *But it must be decided peacefully,* or remain a source of hostile legislation, or perhaps of hostility of a still more serious nature; and if it is so decided, by this tribunal alone can the decision be made. On the Supreme Court of the United States has the Constitution of our country devolved this important duty.

b. "Judicial Restraint: Majoritarianism as Ideal"

Placed in a separate category, for the following reasons, is Justice Felix Frankfurter. His opinions in the apportionment cases of *Colegrove* and *Baker*, exemplify the jurist's primary concern for the continued respect and

---

* On the other hand, Fortas could be classified as a "marginal majoritarian" because he did not think that "one man, one vote" should be extended down to the local political subdivision level.

viability of the Supreme Court in the American Federal system. "The Court's authority," he said in *Baker*, "possessed of neither the purse nor the sword—ultimately rests on sustained public confidence in its moral sanction. Such feeling must be nourished by the Court's complete detachment, in fact and in appearance, from political entanglements and by abstanetion from injecting itself into the clash of political forces in political settlements." The Court, by entering the political thicket, disregards the inherent limits of its power. Frankfurter saw the Court as an anachronism; an oligarchic tribunal in a representative democracy; he was always fearful that the Court would usurp the legitimate powers and responsibilities of the state and federal legislatures and executives.

While his voting pattern is similar to Justice Harlan's, Frankfurter expressed a degree of commitment to the ideal of "majoritarianism" as a standard for representative government. Frankfurter's view of past history and of contemporary America, however, led him to the belief that "one man, one vote" had never really been implemented; that states had always weighted votes based upon geography, interests, etc., and that if the voters wanted to change the system by which seats were apportioned, they had to work through the "blatant" political processes and "sear the conscience" of the legislators in order to bring about the changes demanded.

c. *"Interest Group Representation: Judicial Activism"*

Justices Clark and Stewart maintained emphatically that numerical equality of representation was not constitutionally required. They favored the political philosophy of "group representation" in that they felt that a "proper

diffusion of political initiative as between the thinly populated counties and those having concentrated masses" was
a rational, hence constitutional, state policy. Representative government meant interest group representation; it
did not mean representation based on population. In their
opinions and in their off-the-bench remarks about the
apportionment issue, there was a fear of the concentrated
urban masses—"the bugaboo of majority tyranny" fear—
clearly expressed, most especially in the 1964 cases.

Their political philosophy did include the normative
assertion that the Courts should enter the reapportionment controversy if no other agency of government—
legislative or executive—could act to remove actions and
deeds that violated the prerequisites of representative government as described in the Constitution of the United
States. They both maintained that the Fourteenth Amendment prohibited "invidious state discrimination," and
they felt that if a state apportionment scheme had a
"crazy quilt" pattern exhibiting no rational state policy,
the courts were obliged to enter the conflict.

As Clark stated in *Baker*: "if there were any other relief
available to the people of Tennessee, I would not consider intervention by this Court into so delicate a field."
But there were no remedies available to resolve the constitutional conflict *other than* the judiciary; the Court's
entry into the issue was, in Clark's and Stewart's view,
"in the greatest tradition of this Court."

The major and critical distinction between this conception of representative government and the "majoritarian" conception was that the former conception would
allow judicial intervention *only when* a state apportionment plan was clearly irrational in that there was no
clear cut plan that awarded seats to rural counties and

denied seats to urban counties. This is clearly seen by viewing the Scalogram; the two justices voted for the individual only when the existence of a "crazy quilt" pattern was proven.* To Clark and Stewart, if there appeared a rational pattern of apportionment which denied the principle of equal representation for equal numbers of people, the Court should not intervene by developing and then applying a "rigid constitutional doctrine such as "one man, one vote."

d. *"Interest Group Representation: Judicial Abstention"*

Justice Harlan's primary concern in all these apportionment cases, as seen in the consistent pattern on the Scalogram, was to counter the majoritarianism and judicial activism commitments of his fellow justices. Harlan maintained that electoral disparities must be allowed, that the rigidity of the apportionment formulas (Tennessee's and Alabama's had not been altered in over sixty years) was a definite legislative policy that was rational, that is, such rigidity would ensure against urban interests taking over the state legislature by the sheer weight of population, and that a state could do anything it wanted to in the area of state and congressional apportionment in order to limit the representativeness of the urban masses. Harlan's opinions exhibited a thoroughgoing anti-majoritarianism and the thought of urban majorities gaining control of state legislatures was anathema to the justice— (and he expressed this view in private talks with the author).

---

* *In Swann v. Adams*, the 1967 Florida reapportionment case, it seems that Justice Stewart did not perceive the Florida redistricting plan to be a "crazy quilt" pattern deserving of judicial condemnation.

In addition to his antimajoritarianism, Harlan's opinions reflected his commitment to the principles of separation of power and federalism. Paralleling the views of Frankfurter, Harlan maintained that Court involvement in the apportionment controversy "saps the political process" and "encourages popular inertia"; it weakens the fabric of federalism and places in jeopardy the effectiveness of the Court.

His conception of representative government was, in sum, that the state legislatures were free to create their own form of apportionment (subject only to the Guaranty Clause of the Constitution—and whatever actions the Congress would want to take) and that the Court's entry into this area was a most shameful event in that it violated the cardinal tenets of the separation of powers and the meaning of federalism.

II. "FALLIBILISM" AND "MAJORITARIANISM"

An answer to the question posed at the end of Chapter 1—has "fallibilism" as a concept of democracy been employed, consciously or unconsciously, by the Supreme Court judges?—can be attempted at this point. Thomas Thorson's absolutely binding and universal political recommendation, useful in all contexts with respect to the governing of men, was this: Do not block the way of inquiry and of change with regard to social and economic matters.

Blocking inquiry and change in a democratically oriented institutional setting means restricting the free expression of ideas and the ability to elect representatives who would possibly bring fresh ideas into the political processes. Such action signifies a rejection of the democratic ideal. As Hannah Pitkin wrote, with respect to the twin components of representation (the substantive "ideal" or principle itself and the formal, institutional components): "no institutional arrangement can guarantee the substance, the ideal of representation; yet without institutionalization the ideal remains impotent."[3] Any organization, agent, or general system that blocked a minority or a series of minorities from participating in the political processes was acting in a manner antithetical to the ideal of representative democracy as described by Thorson and others.

The Supreme Court conceptions of democracy developed in the apportionment cases have presented various interpretations of representative government and political equality. Only one of these conceptions developed, the "one man, one vote" or "majoritarian" opinions, reflect and unconsciously employ the fallibilistic conception of democracy. Except for the majoritarian view of democracy, all the normative commitments opt for various degrees of blockage on the part of entrenched power holders.

The "one man, one vote" standard reflects the justices' commitment to the ideas of maximum individual political equality and freedom. (As one scholar has said, the standard is justified *just because* it contributes to the acquisition of these goals.[4]) While the majoritarian view does not maintain that a drastic change will come about in the area of public policy, itself an aspect of the conception of fallibilism, it does maintain that any artificial and intentional actions on the part of minorities to block the political movement of other minorities violates the ideal of democracy and of representative government and diminishes the prospects for political equality and freedom.

Justice Douglas has aptly expressed, in his own words, the ideal of fallibilism and the responsibility of the justices to act where constitutionally protected rights have been impaired, diluted, or blocked by political actors. He said: "Since we live on earth, not in heaven, we will always be imperfect. . . . Whether the decisions were right or wrong, it is the role of the judiciary to make pronouncements, whatever the climate of public opinion."[5] In a recent Supreme Court decision, Douglas wrote that "the problems of government are practical ones. . . . What is best is not always discernible; the wisdom of any choice may be disputed or condemned."[6]

By holding to this view, as the Court majorities in the apportionment cases have done, they have acted rationally, for in addition to the standards of legal and political rationality discussed in Chapter 1 (to be summarized below), Thorson suggests that *rationality consists in deciding wisely in terms of the context of the situation.*[7] Rationality is also a term of commendation[8] and the majority opinions, because there was

(1) weighing the evidence
(2) examination of the political situations existing in the various states
(3) asking and answering of empirical questions
(4) development of a conception of democracy and of representative government that reflected a commitment to the principle of equal numbers of people getting equal numbers of representatives (itself an ideal that is not grounded in absolutist-theocratic terminology but reflects the fallibility of all humans),

did decide wisely and commendably in terms of the situational context.

III. THE QUESTION OF RATIONALITY CONTINUED

In establishing these new legal and political relationships in the apportionment cases, the Court majority did act reasonably and rationally. "Rationality," as Abraham Kaplan wrote recently, "does not require that we know everything, but only that we make the best use of what knowledge we have or can get."[9]

As already indicated, the Court majority in the apportionment cases did make the best uses of the knowledge they possessed and that they did act wisely in the context of the situation.

Regarding standards of political rationality, the Supreme Court, as part of the American "hybrid" political system Robert Dahl wrote about ("the evolution of a political system in which all the active and legitimate groups in the population can make themselves heard at some crucial stage in the process of decision,"),[10] has played a very important role by allowing the complaints of those whose vote was debased by the malapportioned systems to be voiced and acted upon at a crucial stage in the political process.

At a crucial stage, the Court acted favorably on these complaints. In doing so, the justices may very well have changed people's attitudes toward the democratic process. Charles Black wrote recently that "it may be that the most important thing of all (about representation) is that the people feel adequately represented," and that "more and more politically conscious people had come to feel . . . that the representation given them, particularly in State governments was a sham. These [apportionment] decisions, when implemented, ought to dispel that feeling."[11] (This point will shortly be raised again.)

This has not been a new role for the Supreme Court in our history. As C. Herman Pritchett points out: "The Supreme Court has never been detached from the major political issues of our times."[12] From Chief Justice John Marshall's time to the present, successive Courts have been involved in the question of national supremacy and state's rights, economic interests of the various sections of the country, slavery, territorial expansion, civil war, economic expansion and economic liberty, the extent and degree to which the powers of government can be used to prevent depressions and to threaten individual freedoms—social, economic, cultural and political. So it seems that the Supreme Court, "realizing that perhaps like nine Br'er Rabbits they have historically thrived in that briar patch,"[13] is acting rationally when it enters still another controversy regarding the nature and meaning of representative government.

The other standard of rationality mentioned in Chapter 1 was the legal standard. Stressed in that chapter was the notion of the "open-ended texture" of the law whereby standards of conduct must be weighed in the light of changing environmental situations. "The law," wrote Morris R. Cohen, "is a growing and self-correcting system. It grows, not of itself, but by the interaction between social usage and the work of legislatures, courts, and administration officials.[14] The historic task of the Court, and a standard of rationality evidenced in the "majoritarian" opinions, has been to engage in "critical morality," that is, to engage in, when called for, criticism of actual political institutions,[15] using as a standard the Constitution of the United States.

Their task, the judiciary's task generally, has been the "adaptation and adjustment" of the law. Their pronouncements, in the words of Justice Benjamin N. Cardozo, are tentative approximations, "to be judged through their wordings, by some pragmatic sense of truth. . . . We judges grope and feel our way. What we hand down is an hypothesis. It is no longer a divine command."[16] In the apportionment cases, these majoritarian opinions have wrestled with the nature and meaning of terms in the law of the Constitution and have, to the best of their empirical ability, tentatively asserted a constitutional standard regarding the issue of political equality which they feel incorporates the ideal of "Equal Protection of the Laws."

Edmond Cahn wrote that the judge's most difficult task is to "adjust moral standards to the level that society can best aspire to attain." In a sense, both the political and legal standards of rationality point to this task; for rationality in politics and law can be seen as the maintenance of the general social system. By superimposing democratic standards and ideals over democratic reality, and trying to bridge the gap between the two, the Court majority, in an ultimate sense, was acting rationally. The discussion therefore turns to the "objective sought" by the majoritarians; for "the teleology of decision-making is more powerful than its logic in shaping the course of decision."[17]

IV. THE SUPREME COURT: GUARDIAN OF SOCIETY'S DEMOCRATIC VALUES

One scholar has recently suggested that "perhaps, in an increasingly secular society, the Supreme Court serves as a generally accepted moral critic. . . . [Their recent actions] may indicate an unconscious awareness on the part of the justices that in a time of increased moral relativity there should be one section of a secular order which provides some firm guides to conduct."[18] It is suggested, in what has been already described and in what will be discussed below, that the Court's actions support the contention that there was a sincere judicial concern about the separation that existed between democratic theory and empirical reality.

William Riker has commented that the "real problem of democracy . . . is the difference between democratic promise and democratic performance. Its task is to narrow the gap between the real and the ideal, to make the picture for our eyes as pretty as the picture in our heads. . . . Democratic statesmen ought always to try to make government democratic in fact as well as in name. It is a difficult mission."[19]

A host of writers on the contemporary crises of society have commented in this same fashion. Chambers and Salisbury write that the focal problem of democracy today "stems from an apparent contemporary sense of discrepancy between ideal and practice. . . . This involves a perception of a gap between an exalted picture of democracy we inherit from our Western tradition on the one hand, and the reality of democracy as we see it today on the other."[20]

Charles Frankel, writing of the prospects of democracy in the twentieth century, said:[21]

[Men become convinced of the worth of a social system] through its capacity to exemplify a vision of human possibility and to move towards that vision. . . . Democracy must give men something in which to believe . . . and the point about it . . . is that it rests on the assumption that men have some choice [in moving the society toward an identifiable and desired direction], that it is not given to them or prearranged for them, but that, within limits, they can define it for themselves.

Frankel believes that the sense of direction in contemporary America is "most obviously absent." There is an aimlessness, a "rolling with the punches" feeling that is evident among the people. "Disillusioned with the classical metaphor of democracy, we still appear to want" or need some shorthand (though poetic or evocative) statement which, in reasonable accord with the facts, justifies and explains our way of doing things, which gives us some sense of direction."[22]

In the apportionment cases the "majoritarian" justices' major task, one that they were obligated to carry out by their swearing an oath to support the Constitution and to do justice to rich and poor alike, was the protection of the democratic character of the political processes. As Chief Justice Warren wrote: "The issue . . . is not the individual against society; it is, rather, the wise accommodation of the necessities of physical survival with the requirements of spiritual survival. . . . Our system faces no theoretical dilemma but a single continuous problem: how to apply to ever-changing conditions the never-changing principles of freedom."[23] Seen in this objective of the Warren majority is an understanding that the basic values of democracy and of representative government *must* be preserved and, further, that the institutions of government in a democracy *must*—if the system of representative government in a democracy is to continue to exist as a viable one—accommodate themselves to these ideals—as best as is humanly possible.

It is in giving people something viable to believe in that the Court is playing its major role. As Warren's statement, and the majoritarianism opinions indicate, some justices are aware of the crises in values and, as seen in the apportionment cases, are *attempting* "to make American life accord with the noble ideals we Americans profess."[24] In attempting to update the individualistic credo of the political leaders of the Eighteenth Century and adapt it to the pluralism of American society in the twentieth century, the Court majorities have acted rationally.

In elevating the "one man, one vote" concept as a basic constitutional requisite of representative government, the "majoritarians" were attempting to have state legislators act to narrow the gap between theory and reality. Contrary to the dissenters, who wanted to maintain a latter-day version of the "concurrent majority" theory of John C. Calhoun (whereby government acts with the consent of those interest groups affected by the legislation, rather than acting by simple majority rule), the majority opinions, aware of the reality of contemporary life, acted in a reasonable fashion.

The primary role of the Supreme Court, as seen in this examination of the apportionment cases, has been to maintain the ideals the American society has been committed to since our inception as a sovereign state. Its actions have been rational because, in carrying out this task of accommodation and adjustment, it has followed standards of legal and political rationality; has been tentative and open-ended in its decisions, and it has been aware of the human situation which rules out infallibility. This is a difficult and controversial task, but one that should be attempted if the society is to remain committed to the ideals of democracy. Contrary to the views of the dissenters, the opinions of the "majoritarians" have strengthened the institutions of democracy; the "fabric of federalism" may very well have been revived by the "one man, one vote" ideal.

V. COMMENTS ON THE EVALUATION

Some final comments have to be made on another question that has been raised in Chapter 1: whether or not an evaluation of this type can be undertaken, ascertaining the conceptions of democracy and determining the reasonableness of the opinions, when the judges are not professional moral philosophers but, rather, nine harried men with precious little time to reflect on the eternal verities. The tentative answer is in the affirmative.

It has been already pointed out that standards of political and legal rationality have been used as the primary guide in the evaluation. Central in this task of evaluating judicial actions has been the conception of "fallibilism" in the Ideal of Democracy. Rationality, assuming the fallibilistic notion, also means deciding wisely in the situational context the Court finds itself in—on the basis of "open-endedness" in the law and open-endedness in man's knowledge of himself and other humans.

To use the words of a contemporary social philosopher, Adrienne Koch, the actions of the Court majorities in the apportionment cases exhibit three components that parallel Western philosophical thought: (1) a conscious, reasoned examination of their own and society's beliefs and values (with an appraisal of their validity and continued viability), (2) the integration of beliefs that have been critically appraised, that is, the ability of the agent to incorporate new facets of knowledge into the decision-making operation, and (3) a demonstration by the agent that he shows a basic central concern with, and places a high value on, the root values of the society and the individual in his larger community.

In the apportionment cases, the "majoritarians" did present a prolonged (from *Baker* to *Kirkpatrick*), reasoned, and reasonable examination of the nature and viability of the Ideals of Representative Government, Democracy, Political Equality. They did critically appraise the existential situation in the American states, the particular cases involved—Tennessee, Georgia, Alabama, New York, Colorado, Virginia, Maryland, Delaware, Florida, Missouri, Texas, Michigan, Hawaii—and they did integrate the standard they found to be apposite: "one man, one vote." And certainly, the Supreme Court majority showed a basic concern, and placed a high value on the root values of the society—that is, representative government in an operational democracy. While not professional moral philosophers, the majority of the justices did exhibit, in their discussions and in their opinions, reflective, critical tendencies when they examined the questions put before them in the apportionment controversy. Therefore, using Koch's criteria, one would conclude that the Supreme Court is part of the mainstream of Western political thought insofar as its actions in the apportionment controversy are concerned.

NOTES: CHAPTER SIX

1. Glendon Schubert, "The Study of Judicial Decision-Making As An Aspect of Political Behavior" LII *American Political Science Review,* Dec. 1958, p. 1014.

2. George A. Belknap, "A Method For Analyzing Legislative Behavior" 11 *Midwest Journal of Political Science*, Nov. 1958, p. 383.
3. Hannah Pitkin, *Representation*, New York, Atherton Press, 1969, p. 22.
4. Martin Shapiro, *Law and Politics In the Supreme Court*, Glencoe, Free Press, 1964, p. 244.
5. William O. Douglas, "The Bill of Rights Is Not Enough," in Edmond Cahn, *The Great Rights*, New York, Macmillan Co., 1963, pp. 121–22.
6. *Metropolis Theatre v. Chicago*, 228 *US* 61, at 69–70.
7. Thorson, *The Logic of Democracy*, pp. 83, ff.
8. Paul Freund, "Rationality in Judicial Decisions", in Friedrich, *op cit.*, p. 110.
9. In Friedrich, *op cit.*, p. 58.
10. Robert Dahl, *A Preface To Democratic Theory*, Chicago, University of Chicago Press, 1956, pp. 137–318.
11. In J. Roland Pennock and John Chapman, editors, *Representation*, Nomos X, New York, Atherton Press, 1968, p. 142.
12. "Equal Protection and the Urban Majority," LVIII *American Political Science Review*, No. 4, December 1964, p. 869.
13. Walter Murphy, "Deeds Under A Doctrine," LIX *American Political Science Review*, March 1965, page 67.
14. *Reason and Law*, Glencoe, The Free Press, 1950, p. 75–76.
15. H. L. A. Hart, *Law, Liberty and Morality*, Stanford, Stanford University Press, 1963, pp. 2–3.
16. Benjamin Cardozo, *Law and Literature*, New York, Harcourt, Brace & Co., 1931, p. 15, 17.
17. Thomas Cowan, "Decision Theory In Law, Science and Technology" 17 *Rutgers Law Review*, Spring 1963, pp. 499–509.
18. Sigler, *op cit.*, p. 228.
19. Riker, *op cit.*, p. 34.
20. William Chamber and Robert Salisbury, *Democracy Today, Problems And Prospects*, New York, Collier Books, 1962, p. 12.
21. Frankel, *op cit.*, p. 178–179.
22. Chamber and Salisbury, *op cit.*, p. 14.
23. Earl Warren, "The Law," *op cit.*, p. 10.
24. Alpheus T. Mason and William M. Beaney, *The Supreme Court In A Free Society*, New York, W. W. Norton and Co., 1968, p. 322.
25. Adrienne Koch, *Philosophy For A Time Of Crisis*, New York, Dutton, 1959, pp. 58, 60–62, ff.

Bibliography

Advisory Commission on Intergovernmental Relations, *Apportionment of State Legislatures,* Washington, D.C., U.S. Government Printing Office, Dec. 1962.

Aiken, Henry David, *Reason and Conduct, New Bearings in Moral Philosophy,* New York: A. Knopf, 1962.

Auerbach, Carl, "The Reapportionment Cases: One Person, One Vote: One Vote, One Value." in Philip Kurland, editor, *The Supreme Court Review,* 1964, Chicago: University of Chicago Press, 1964.

Bachrach, Peter, *The Theory of Democratic Elitism: A Critique,* Boston: Little, Brown & Co., 1967.

Baker, Gordon E., *The Politics of Reapportionment in Washington,* New York, Holt, Rinehart & Winston, Inc., 1960.

Baker, Gordon, *The Reapportionment Revolution,* New York: Random House, 1965.

Barker, Ernest, *Principles of Social and Political Theory,* New York: Oxford University Press, 1951.

Bay, Christian, "Politics and Pseudopolitics," LIX *American Political Science Review,* March 1965.

Bazelon, David, *The Paper Economy,* New York: Random House, 1963.

Belknap, George M., "A Method for Analyzing Legislative Behavior," 2 *Midwest Journal of Political Science,* Nov. 1958.

Benn, S. I. and Peters, R. S., *Social Principles and the Democratic State,* London: George Allen and Unwin, 1959.

Benson, Oliver, *Political Science Laboratory,* Columbus, Ohio: Charles Merrill Co., 1968.

Berry, Brian and Meltzer, Jack, editors, *Goals For Urban America,* Englewood Cliffs: Prentice-Hall, 1967.

241

Bickel, Alexander M., *Politics and The Warren Court*, New York: Harper & Row, 1955, 1965.

Black, Hugo L., *A Constitutional Faith*, New York: Alfred A. Knopf, 1968.

Blair, George, *American Legislatures: Structure and Process*, New York: Harper & Row, 1967.

Boskoff, Alvin and Ziegler, Harmon, *Voting Patterns In A Local Election*, New York: Lippincott and Co., 1964.

Boulding, Kenneth, "Social Justice in Social Dynamics," in Richard Brant, editor, *Social Justice*, Englewood Cliffs, Prentice-Hall, 1962.

Boyd, William, *Changing Patterns of Apportionment*, New York: National Municipal League, 1965.

Brinton, Crane, *The Anatomy of Revolution*, New York: Vintage Books, 1965.

Cahn, Edmond, *The Moral Decision, Right and Wrong in the Light of American Law*, Bloomington: Indiana University Press, 1955.

———, *The Predicament of Democratic Man*.

Cardozo, Benjamin, *Law and Literature*, New York: Harcourt, Brace and Co., 1931.

Cohen, Felix S., *The Legal Conscience*, New Haven: Yale University Press, 1960.

Cohen, Morris R., *Ethical Systems and Legal Ideals*, Ithaca: Cornell University Press, 1959.

———, *Reason and Law*, Glencoe: The Free Press, 1950.

Congressional Quarterly Weekly Review, "Metropolitan Areas Face Severe Governmental Problems," XIV August 25, 1961.

Connolly, William E., ed., *The Bias of Pluralism*, New York: Atherton Press, 1969.

Cowan, Thomas, "Decision Theory in Law, Science, and Technology," 17 *Rutgers Law Review*, Spring 1963.

Crane, Wilder, "Inertia in the Courts—Tennessee," in Malcolm Jewell, editor, *The Politics of Reapportionment*, New York: Atherton Press, 1964.

David, Paul and Eisenberg, Ralph, *Devaluation of the Urban and Suburban Vote*, Charlottesville, University of Virginia Press, 1961.

Dahl, Robert, *A Preface To Democratic Theory*, Chicago: University of Chicago Press, 1956.

————, *Modern Political Analysis*, Englewood Cliffs: Prentice-Hall, 1963.

————, *Pluralistic Democracy in the United States*, Chicago: Rand-McNally Co., 1967.

Derge, David, "The Lawyer in the Indiana General Assembly," VI *Midwest Journal of Political Science*, February 1962.

Derge, David, "Urban-Rural Conflict: The Case In Illinois," in Wahlke and Eulau, editor, *Legislative Behavior: A Reader in Theory and Research*, Glencoe: Free Press, 1960.

Dixon, Robert G., Jr., "Reapportionment in the Supreme Court and Congress," 63 *Michigan Law Review*, No. 2, Dec. 1964.

Douglas, William O., Jr., "The Bill of Rights is Not Enough," in Edmond Cahn, editor, *The Great Rights*, New York: Macmillan Co., 1963.

————, "The Public Trial and a Free Press," 46 *American Bar Association Journal*, August 1960.

Dye, Thomas, "Malapportionment and Public Policy," XXVII *Journal of Politics*, August 1964.

Edel, Abraham, *Ethical Judgment*, Glencoe: Free Press, 1955.

————, *Science and the Structure of Ethics*, Chicago: University of Chicago, 1961.

Ehrmann, Henry, editor, *Democracy in a Changing Society*, New York: Praeger and Co., 1964.

Elazar, Daniel, *American Federalism: A View From the States*, New York: Thomas Crowell and Co., 1966.

Fein, Leonard, editor, *American Democracy*, New York: Random House, 1965.

Frankel, Charles, *The Democratic Prospect*, New York: Harper and Co., 1962.

Frankfurter, Felix, *Of Law and Men*, New York: Harcourt, Brace and Co., 1956.

Freund, Paul, "Rationality in Judicial Decisions," in Carl Friedrich, editor, *Nomos VII: Rational Decision*, New York: Atherton Press, 1964.

Friedman, Robert, "The Urban-Rural Conflict Revisited," 14 *Western Political Quarterly*, 1961.

Friedmann, W., *Law in a Changing Society*, Baltimore: Penguin Books, 1964.

Fuller, Lon, *Legal Fictions*, Stanford: Stanford University Press, 1967.

————, *The Law in Quest of Itself*, Cambridge: Harvard University Press, 1962.

Ginsberg, Morris, *On Justice In Society*, Baltimore: Penguin Books, 1965.

Girvetz, Harry, editor, *Democracy and Elitism*, New York: Scribner's Sons, 1967.

Goldberg, Arthur, "Gideon's Trumpet: The Poor Man and the Laws," *CBS Reports Transcript*, October 7, 1964.

Grimes, Allan P., *Equality in America*, New York: Oxford University Press, 1964.

Hacker, Andrew, *Congressional Districting*, Washington, D.C., Brookings Institute, 1964.

Hamilton, Howard, editor, *Legislative Reapportionment*, New York: Harper and Row, 1964.

————, "Legislative Reapportionment in Indiana: Some Observations and a Suggestion," 35 *Notre Dame Lawyer*, May 1960.

Hand, Learned, *The Spirit of Liberty*, New York: Vintage Books, 1959.

Hanson, Royce, *The Political Thicket*, Englewood Cliffs: Prentice-Hall, 1966.

Hart, H. L. A., *Law, Liberty and Morality*, Stanford: Stanford University Press, 1963.

————, *The Concept of Law*, London: Oxford University Press, 1961.

Hartz, Louis, *The Liberal Tradition in America*, New York: Harcourt, Brace and Co., 1955.

Harvard, William C. and Beth, Loren P., *The Politics of Misrepresentation*, Baton Rouge: Louisiana State University Press, 1962.

Hawkins, Brett and Whelchel, Cheryl, "Reapportionment and Urban Representation In Legislative Influence Positions: The Case of Georgia," 3 *Urban Affairs Quarterly*, March 1968.

Hill, A. Spencer, "The Reapportionment Decisions: A Return To Dogma?" 31 *Journal of Politics*, Feb. 1969.

Hofferbert, Richard I., "The Relation Between Public Policy and Some Structural and Environmental Variables in the American States," 60 *American Political Science Review*, No. 1, March 1966.

Hofstadter, Richard, *The Age of Reform*, New York: Random House, 1955.

Howard, J. Woodford, Jr., "On the Fluidity of Judicial Choice," LXII *American Political Science Review*, March 1968.

Irwin, William P., "Reapportionment and Representation: Search For A Theory," in Howard Hamilton, editor, *Reapportioning Legislatures*, Columbus: Charles E. Merrill Books, 1966.

Israel, Jerold, "On Charting A Course Through The Mathematical Quagmire: The Future of Baker v. Carr," 61 *Michigan Law Review*, No. 1, November 1962.

Jewell, Malcolm, "Constitutional Provisions for State Legislative Apportionment," *Western Political Quarterly*, June 1955.

———, *The Politics of Apportionment*, New York: Atherton Press, 1965.

———, *The State Legislature*, New York: Random House, 1955.

Johnson, Richard M., *The Dynamics of Compliance*, Evanston: Northwestern University Press, 1967.

Jones, Victor, "American Local Government in a Changing Federalism," 11 *American Review*, May 1962.

Kaplan, Abraham, "Some Limitations on Rationality," in Carl Friedrich, *Nomos VII: Rational Decision*, New York: Atherton Press, 1965.

Kauper, Paul, "Some Comments on the Reapportionment Cases," 63 *Michigan Law Review*, September 1964.

Klain, Maurice, "A New Look at the Constituencies; The Need For a Recount and a Reappraisal," 49 *American Political Science Review*, No. 4, Dec. 1955.

Koch, Adrienne, *Philosophy For a Time of Crisis*, New York: E. P. Dutton and Co., 1959.

Krinsky, Fred, Democracy and Complexity: *Who Governs The Governors?* Beverley Hills: The Glencoe Press, 1968.

Ladd, John, "The Place of Practical Reason in Judicial Decision," in Carl Friedrich, *Nomos VII: Rational Decision*.

Lamb, Karl, "Michigan Legislative Apportionment: Key to Constitutional Change," in Malcolm Jewell, editor, *The Politics of Reapportionment*, New York: Atherton Press, 1965.

Lasswell, Harold, "Psychology Looks at Morals and Politics," *Ethics*, April 1941.

Lerman, Allan and Chase, Harold, editors, *Kennedy and the Press*, New York: Thomas Crowell Co., 1965.

Levi, Edward, *An Introduction To Legal Reasoning*, Chicago: University of Chicago Press, 1948.

Levy, Leonard, ed., *Judicial Review and The Supreme Court*, New York: Harper & Row, 1967.

Lewis, Anthony, "A Passionate Concern," *The New York Times*, February 24, 1965.

————, "Legislative Apportionment and the Federal Courts," 71 *Harvard Law Review*, April 1958.

Lloyd, Dennis, *The Idea of Law*, Baltimore: Penguin Books, 1964.

Lockhard, Duane, *Connecticut's Challenge Primary: A Study in Legislative Politics*, Eagleton Institute Cases in Practical Politics, Number 7, New York: McGraw-Hill, 1960.

————, *The Politics of State and Local Government*, New York: Macmillan, 1963.

Lukas, J. Anthony, "Barnyard Government in Maryland," *The Reporter*, April 12, 1962.

Lytle, Clifford, *The Warren Court and Its Critics*, Tucson: University of Arizona Press, 1968.

Mason, Alpheus and Beaney, William, *The Supreme Court In A Free Society*, New York: W. W. Norton and Co., 1968.

McCloskey, Robert, "The Reapportionment Case," 76 *Harvard Law Review*, November 1962.

McDonald, Neil, *Politics: A Study of Control Behavior*, New Brunswick: Rutgers University Press, 1965.

McKay, Robert, *Reapportionment: The Law and Politics of Equal Representation*, New York: Twentieth Century Fund, 1965.

Meehan, Eugene, *Contemporary Political Thought: A Critical Appraisal*, Homewood: Dorsey Press, 1967.

————, *Value Judgment and Social Science*, Homewood: Dorsey Press, 1969.

Mitau, G. Theodore, *Decade of Decision: The Supreme Court and the Constitutional Revolution, 1954–1964*, New York: Charles Scribner's Sons, 1967.

Murphy, Walter, "Deeds Under A Doctrine," LIX *American Political Science Review*, December 1964.

————, *Elements of Judicial Strategy*, Chicago: University of Chicago Press, 1965.

Murphy, Walter and Pritchett, C. Herman, editors, *Courts, Judges, and Politics*, New York: Random House, 1961.

Myrdal, Gunnar, *An American Dilemma, Two Volumes*, New York: McGraw-Hill, 1964.

Olafson, Frederick A., editor, *Justice and Social Policy*, Englewood Cliffs: Prentice-Hall, 1961.

Padover, Saul K., editor, *To Secure These Blessings: The Great Debates of The Constitutional Convention of 1787*, New York: Ridge Press, 1962.

Pennock, J. Roland and Chapman, John W., ed., *Representation, Nomos X*, New York: Atherton Press, 1968.

Perelman, Charles, *The Idea of Justice and the Problem of Argument*, New York: Humanities Press, 1963.

Pitkin, Hannah, ed., *Representation*, New York: Atherton Press, 1969.

Pritchett, C. Herman, "Equal Protection and The Urban Majority," 58 *American Political Science Review*, No. 4, Dec. 1964.

Reimer, Neil, ed., *The Representative: Trustee? Delegate? Partisan? Politico?*, Boston: D.C. Heath & Co., 1967.

————, *The Revival of Democratic Theory*, New York: Appleton Century Crofts, 1962.

Riker, William, *Democracy In the United States,* New York: Macmillan and Co., 1965.

Sandifer, Durward and Scheman, L. Ronald, *The Foundations of Freedom,* New York: Praeger and Co., 1965.

Saye, Albert, "The Precedent Setter," 54 *National Municipal Review,* September 1965.

Schattschneider, E. E., *The Semi-Sovereign People,* New York: Holt, Rinehart and Co., 1960.

Schmidhauser, John R., *Iowa's Campaign for a Constitutional Convention in 1960,* Eagleton Institute Cases in Practical Politics, Number 30, New York: McGraw-Hill, 1963.

Schubert, Glendon, *Judicial Behavior: A Reader in Behavior and Research,* Chicago: Rand-McNally Co., 1964.

———, *Judicial Policy-Making,* Chicago: Scott-Foresman Co., 1965.

———, *Reapportionment,* New York: Charles Scribner's Sons, 1965.

———, "The Study of Judicial Decision-Making As An Aspect of Political Behavior," LII *American Political Science Review,* No. 4, Dec. 1958.

Schuman, Samuel, *Legal Positivism,* Detroit: Wayne State University Press, 1961.

Shapiro, Martin, *Freedom of Speech: The Supreme Court and Judicial Review,* Englewood Cliffs: Prentice-Hall, 1966.

———, *Law and Politics In The Supreme Court,* Glencoe: The Free Press, 1965.

Sharkansky, Ira, "Voting Behavior of Metropolitan Congressmen: Prospects For Changes With Reapportionment," 28 *Journal of Politics,* Nov. 1966.

Sibley, Milford Q., "The Limitations of Behavioralism," in James Charlesworth, editor, *Contemporary Political Analysis,* Glencoe: The Free Press, 1967.

Sigler, Jay A., *An Introduction To The Legal System,* Homewood: Dorsey Press, 1968.

Silva, Ruth C., "Compared Values of the Single and the Multi-Member Legislative District," *Western Political Quarterly,* Sept. 1964.

———, "Legislative Reapportionment—With Special Reference To New York," XXVII *Law and Contemporary Problems,* Summer 1962.

Sorauf, Frank, *Party and Representation,* New York: Atherton Press, 1963.

Sorokin, Pitirim, *The Crisis of Our Age,* New York: E. P. Dutton, 1941.

Spitz, David, *Patterns of Anti-Democratic Thought,* New York: The Free Press, 1949, 1965.

Street, Harry, *Freedom, The Individual, and the Law,* Baltimore: Penguin Books, 1963.

Strout, Richard, "The Next Election Is Rigged," *Harper's Magazine,* November 1959.

Sutherland, Arthur, *Constitutionalism In America,* New York: Blaisdell Publishing Co., 1965.

Thompson, Kirk, "Constitutional Theory and Political Action," 31 *Journal of Politics,* August 1969.

Thorson, Thomas, "Epilogue to Absolute Majority Rule," 23 *Journal of Politics,* August 1961.

————, *The Logic of Democracy,* New York: Holt, Rinehart and Winston, 1962.

Tinder, Glenn, *The Crisis of Political Imagination,* New York: Charles Scribner's Sons, 1964.

Toulmin, Stephen, *An Examination of the Place of Reason In Ethics,* London: Cambridge University Press, 1950.

Tyler, Gus and Wells, David, "New York: Constitutionally Republican," in Malcolm Jewell, editor, *The Politics of Reapportionment,* New York: Atherton Press, 1965.

United States Commission on Civil Rights, *Report Number One, Voting,* Washington, D. C., 1961.

Warren, Earl, "The Law And The Future," *Fortune Magazine,* November 1955.

West, Ben, *Legislative Apportionment in Tennessee, 1901–1961,* Nashville, Tennessee, 1961.

Index

Alabama, 239
  racial consequences of malapportionment, 64
Apportionment:
  constitutional standards, 164
  core of democratic crisis, 51–52
  democracy, 42–43
  distribution of political power, 52
  genesis of constitutional crisis, 52–53
  gerrymandered districts, 213–214
  judicial perceptions of importance, 25
  judicial test developed by Court, 212
  malapportionment:
    consequences on one-party states, 63–64
    divided control of government, 62–63
    effects, 59
    effect on public policy outputs, 65–66
    major factors accounting for, 53
    racial consequences, 63–65
  mathematical deviations from population ideal, 210
  questions after *Reynolds v Sims*, 183, 199, 215
  "rules of thumb", 183
  special interests benefitted from, 58
  urban self-consciousness, 58
  vital determinant in a democratic system, 43

Avery v Midland County, 204, 206–210

Baker v Carr, 46, 149, 182, 221, 224, 225, 227, 239
  background of Tennessee case, 91–94
  conceptual frameworks developed by Supreme Court justices, 114–120
  evaluation of judicial opinions, 113–129
  Justice Department brief, 92–93
  opinions, 97–113
  pandora's box, 139
Baker, Gordon, 60
Bay, Christian, 44
Black, Charles, 232
Black, Hugo L., 93, 191, 222
  distinguishes First Article from 14th Amendment, 163
  opinion in *Colegrove v Green*, 72–75
  interview with, 163n
  view of democracy, 72–74, 163
Brennan, Jr., William J., 89, 116, 191, 200, 222
  adequacy of his technical evaluation in *Baker v Carr*, 120, 121, 125
  conception of democracy, 96
  majority opinion in *Baker v Carr*, 94–98
  majority opinion in *Kirkpatrick v Preisler*, 211–213

251

LW/

E56 MS

Ball